W9-AYD-680

BENAZIR BHUTTO

BENAZIR BHUTTO

KATHERINE M. DOHERTY

and

CRAIG A. DOHERTY

AN IMPACT BIOGRAPHY

FRANKLIN WATTS

New York London Toronto Sydney 1990

Photographs courtesy of:
AP/Wide World Photos: pp. 32, 35, 47, 61, 77, 85, 101, 123, 131, 134, 135, 138; UPI/Bettmann Newsphotos: p. 44; Reuters/Bettmann Newsphotos: pp. 83, 91, 99; Gamma-Liaison: pp. 111 (Anis Hamdani), 120 (Victoria Brynner), 126 (Shamin ur Rhama).

Library of Congress Cataloging-in-Publication Data

Doherty, Katherine M.
Benazir Bhutto / Katherine M. Doherty and Craig A. Doherty.
p. cm. — (An Impact biography)
Includes bibliographical references.
Summary: A biography of Benazir Bhutto, Pakistan's first woman prime minister with emphasis on the political situation that enabled her to rise to power.
ISBN 0-531-10936-4
1. Bhutto, Benazir—Juvenile literature. 2. Pakistan—Politics and government—1971–1988—Juvenile liturature. 3. Pakistan—Politics and government—1988– —Juvenile literature. 4. Prime ministers—Pakistan—Biography—Juvenile literature. [1. Bhutto, Benazir. 2. Prime ministers. 3. Pakistan—Politics and government—1971–1988. 4. Pakistan—Politics and government—1988–]
I. Doherty, Craig A. II. Title.
DS389.22.B48D64 1990
954.9105'092—dc20
[B]
[92]
90–12289 CIP AC

Printed in the United States of America
6 5 4 3 2 1

Acknowledgments

Many people deserve credit in the production of a book like this, and we would like to publicly acknowledge the contributions of the following people and institutions: thanks to our editors Iris Rosoff and Mary Perrotta, who felt this book should be written; to Meghan Doherty, our daughter, who suffered cheerfully and usually silently throughout our researching and writing of this book; to the New Hampshire Technical College—Berlin, where Katherine is the librarian, for having the technology needed to do much of the research; to Yvonne Thomas and the rest of the efficient and ever-helpful staff at the Berlin (NH) Public Library; to Barbara Barbieri, at the Berlin High School Library; to Amanda MacKinnon, who helped with Meghan while we worked on the book; and to our family and friends for their continued support and encouragement.

Contents

Introduction

The first time that we saw Benazir Bhutto we were greatly impressed by her poise, beauty, and youth. Here was a woman a couple of years younger than us who had lived in Cambridge, Massachusetts, at the same time we did, appearing on the news as the leading opponent of the military dictator General Zia in Pakistan. It was exciting to listen to the accolades the press bestowed upon her. After she had become prime minister and our editor suggested that we do a book about her, we began to look more seriously at the first woman to head a modern Islamic state and the youngest head of state in the world. The more research we did, the more struck we were with the adversity that Benazir Bhutto had faced and overcome in her long struggle with the military powers of Pakistan.

She has inherited her father Zulfikar Ali Bhutto's political legacy and sits as only the second popularly elected head of state in her country's brief history. It is a precarious position, as she well knows. Military coups, assassinations, the exiling of leaders and, in the case of her father, kangaroo court sentences and executions are commonplace in the political arena in which she operates.

The fact that she is a woman adds to the insecurity of her position. Many on Pakistan's religious right feel that women should be restricted to activities within the home. General Zia had done much during his eleven-year reign to reinforce that position. The illiteracy rate among women in Pakistan far exceeds that of men, and the rate at which women die in childbirth is one of the highest in the world. Under Zulfikar Ali Bhutto, women had begun to make gains, but General Zia had erased them.

The other problems her country faces are nearly staggering. Illiteracy and poverty are rampant. The almost feudal relationship that exists between the wealthy land owners—the Bhutto family among them—and their tenants makes the establishment of democratic reforms difficult. Under General Zia, the heroin trade grew into a multimillion dollar industry which has produced over a million heroin addicts in Pakistan. The Zia regime let a number of well-organized drug gangs operate with impunity.

Benazir Bhutto is revered by many people of her country who see her as the natural successor to her now martyred father. But the specter of the military is always present. Only time will tell us if Benazir Bhutto will be able to convert the worship of the people into a viable system of democratic government immune from the ambitions of the military establishment.

BENAZIR BHUTTO

Pakistan: A Culture Divided

Early History

To understand Benazir Bhutto's life and position, you must first know a little bit about the country she governs. Pakistan, on the Arabian Sea, is bordered by Iran, Afghanistan, the Soviet Union, the People's Republic of China, and India. Pakistan's climate ranges from semi-arid to desert and its elevation goes from sea level along the Arabian Sea to 20,000 feet above sea level in the northern mountains. The mountains of Pakistan are the northern reaches of the Himalayas.

Agriculture is extremely important to Pakistan. The waters of the Indus River, which runs through the center of the country, provide the means to irrigate the crops.

Within the borders of Pakistan are the remains of one of the earliest civilizations, yet Pakistan as a country did not exist until 1947. To understand the modern country, some knowledge of the ancient history of the area is important.

Along the banks of the Indus are the ruins of the Harappan culture. This culture flourished five thousand years ago, and archaeologists have determined from the ruins that this culture had a high degree of sophistication. In fact, the residents of Harappan cities like Mohenjo-Daro in Sind Province probably had better sanitation and a higher standard of living than many of the residents of Pakistan today.

Over the next few thousand years, the area that is now Pakistan was carved up, fought over, and marched through by a variety of peoples and empires. Alexander the Great marched eastward as far as the Indus. The Kushan Empire, the Mauryan Empire, and the Imperial Guptas all held sway in Pakistan at one time. Hinduism, Buddhism, Brahmanism, and Tantricism were just some of the religions practiced in the area. It was not until the seventh and eighth centuries A.D. that a unifying force returned to the area.

In the early seventh century, the Prophet Muhammad put forth the teachings that would later be called the religion of Islam. Modern Islam is based on the Quran, the holy book of the Muslims, which contains the revelations of Allah (god) to Muhammad. The Muslims believe that there is only one god (Allah), who spoke to the people through his messenger Muhammad. Muslims, people who believe in Islam, are supposed to pray five times a day facing the holy city of Mecca, where Muhammad was born, which is in Saudi Arabia. Muslims are expected to visit Mecca once in their lifetime.

Within the historically brief time of two hundred years,

the influence of Islam spread westward across northern Africa into Spain and eastward into central Asia. The first incursion into what is today Pakistan occurred in 711, when an Arab expedition invaded Baluchistan and Sind.

Over the next few hundred years, the influence of Islam grew. Muslim teachers spread among the people of the region and paved the way for the Islamic conquest of the subcontinent by Muslims from the Middle East beginning around the year 1000. By 1300 almost all of the subcontinent was under the control of Muslim rulers. Non-Muslims who were willing to pay the jizya, or protection tax, were permitted to practice their own religions. Throughout the subcontinent, Muslims, Hindus, and Buddhists coexisted in a dynamic culture that experienced a period of renaissance in the arts and literature.

Except for the sack of Delhi in 1398 by Tamerlane, the Muslim leaders protected the subcontinent from the Mongol hordes that were conquering much of the rest of the civilized world. However, by the sixteenth century the subcontinent had become so fragmented that the Muslim leaders finally succumbed to invasion from the north.

In 1526, after the first Battle of Panipat, Babur of Fergana controlled the area of the Sultanate of Delhi. Babur and his successors led what is called the Mughal (or Mogul) Empire. During the reign of the Mughal Empire, the subcontinent flourished. But by 1707, the Mughal sun had begun to set.

At about the same time, a new player on the subcontinent appeared. The Europeans, first in the personage of the Portuguese sailor Vasco da Gama, landed on the Malabar coast in 1498. The Portuguese wrested control of the Indian Ocean from the Arabs, and the floodgates of trade were thrown open. Not to be outdone, other European countries—England, France, and Holland—joined the rush to establish trading stations in the Indies. The Dutch East India Company concentrated mainly on the spice trade in what is now Indonesia. The East India Company (British) traded with India as did the French East India Company.

The various regional leaders in India negotiated with the French, English, Dutch, and Portuguese traders with all sides vying for the upper hand on the subcontinent. Robert Clive, in 1757, won the decisive victory for the British East India Company at Plassey when he defeated the Nawab of Bengal, Siraj ud Daula. Clive then defeated the Mughal Emperor Shah Alam at the Battle of Buxar in 1764, and for nearly two hundred years the subcontinent labored under the Union Jack, the flag of Great Britain.

Unlike North and South America, which had a small native population that the Europeans were able to subdue and supplant, the subcontinent was much more of a business venture for the British. The East India Company was interested in only one thing from the colony of India: profit.

To ensure a continuing flow of goods out of India and to increase the markets for the factories of England, the East India Company continued to expand British influence on the subcontinent. Campaign after campaign was fought to acquire more territory. Throughout the first half of the nineteenth century, the company fought for and won additional lands on the subcontinent.

The year 1857 marks a turning point in British-Indian relations. The Indian Mutiny, or Sepoy Rebellion, a revolt by native soldiers in the employ of the East India Company, forced Britain to reevaluate its position in India. The revolt started over the issuing of new Enfield rifles to the troops. These new guns used a cartridge that had to be bitten open before it was inserted into the breech of the rifle. These cartridges were greased, and it was the grease that caused the problem. The Muslim soldiers believed that the grease used was from pig fat; the Hindu soldiers believed it was grease made from cow fat. In either case the thought of inserting the by-product of a forbidden food in one's mouth set off the rebellion.

After the Sepoy Rebellion, England replaced the East India Company with a colonial government directly responsible to Britain's Queen. By unifying India into one political entity, the British planted the seed that would eventually grow into nationalism for India and Pakistan. The Indian National Congress was set up in 1895 to give Indians a forum for expressing their concerns about the governing of the subcontinent.

As the twentieth century began, the feelings of nationalism intensified. The India Councils Act of 1909 gave the people of the subcontinent limited participation in the governing of India. As the British bureaucracy grew, so did the role of Indians in running it. The closer India grew toward autonomy, the more apparent the problems of the minorities became. The largest minority within the territory of British India was the Muslims.

In 1906 the Muslim League was founded to champion the causes of Muslims in India. Over the next forty years the Muslim minority of India, which was most concentrated in the northwestern and the northeastern corners of India, saw themselves more as a community joined by their religion than as a part of the heterogeneous country of India. Out of this feeling grew the idea for a separate Muslim state. In the early 1930s the idea that there should be a separate Muslim state was put forth by Mohammad Iqbal, a Muslim poet. In 1933 a group of Muslim students from the subcontinent who were studying at Cambridge University in England published a pamphlet entitled *Now or Never.* In the pamphlet they supported the idea of a separate Muslim state. They proposed to call this Muslim state *Pakistan,* meaning the land of the Paks, the spiritually pure. The pamphlet also made an anagram of the word "Pakistan" stating that the letters came from the names of the Muslim regions of the area: *P*unjab, *A*fghana (Northwest Frontier Province), *K*ashmir, *I*ran, *S*ind, *T*urkharistan, Afghanistan, Baluchista*n*.

During this time, two organizations led the independence movement. Mohandas K. Gandhi led the Indian National Congress and Mohammad Ali Jinnah led the All-India Muslim League. At times the two groups cooperated in trying to escape the yoke of British colonialism. Often, however, they were in opposition to each other, especially as the movement for a separate Islamic state grew.

Gandhi's congress continued to push for a unified India. The conflict began to grow violent as rioting broke out between Muslims and Hindus. It is interesting to note that in the areas that eventually became East and West Pakistan, where the Muslims held the majority, the league was much less powerful. The greatest problems arose where the minority Muslims feared that they would be discriminated against by the Hindu majority.

By 1945 the end of World War II in Europe and a victory for the Labour Party in England, among other factors, helped make independence for the subcontinent a foregone conclusion. The communal violence between Hindus and Muslims brought the subcontinent to the brink of civil war. The English Lord Louis Mountbatten was sent to India in February 1947 as Viceroy, with instructions from London to transfer power to the Indian people by June of 1948.

Mountbatten assessed the situation and the positions of the factions involved and saw the need to act as quickly as possible. He astutely realized that the Hindu congress would accept partition in exchange for independence. He also saw that Jinnah and the Muslim League would rather take a smaller Pakistan than none at all and the people caught in the middle would learn to live with partition.

On July 14, 1947, the British House of Commons passed the India Independence Act, creating the modern states of Pakistan and India. The summer of 1947 was plagued by drought, floods, and violence, and all sides learned how inadequately prepared they were for independence.

The Nation of Pakistan

On August 7, 1947, Mohammad Ali Jinnah flew from Delhi to Karachi to become the first Governor-General of Pakistan. When Pakistan officially came into existence one week later on August 14, 1947, the problems that Jinnah faced must have seemed nearly insurmountable. He was the head of a country that the day before had not existed. This country was divided into two parts separated by 1600 kilometers (1000 miles). Within a few months, eight million Hindus and Sikhs had left Pakistan, primarily from the Punjab, and six million Muslims had moved to Pakistan from India. In the process 250,000 people died. The Muslim immigrants in Pakistan became known as the *muhajirs*. Within the borders of the newly created country of Pakistan was a variety of ethnic and linguistic groups that have yet to meld together.

Jinnah became the head of a country that had no national identity, no national economy, and no national bureaucracy. Pakistan had lost much of its middle class. It faced the problem of dealing with six million muhajirs, many of whom moved into the few urban areas of West Pakistan. It is estimated that the muhajir population of Karachi and the other West Pakistan cities reached as high as 46 percent in 1951.

Possibly the greatest problem facing Jinnah and Pakistan was the lack of experience in self-government. It had been almost five thousand years since the area of West Pakistan had been an autonomous region. East Pakistan—1,000 miles away across a now hostile India—would have been nearly ungovernable for even the most experienced and efficient.

The newly formed government of Pakistan depended on the British viceregal model with Jinnah as the governor-general. This too created problems in Pakistan as Benazir Bhutto attempted to continue the democratic reforms begun by her father. Jinnah set the precedent for dictatorial rule that opened the door for the succession of military leaders that followed. Of the forty-odd years that Pakistan has existed, the military has ruled for thirty-two years.

Jinnah's term as governor-general was short-lived. After only thirteen months in office, on September 11, 1948, Jinnah died. His positions were divided among his successors, but the real power of the government fell to Jinnah's right-hand man, Liaquat Ali Khan, who became prime minister.

Liaquat attempted to lead Pakistan toward democracy. His experience as a lawyer under British rule in India gave

CHINA
U.S.S.R.
②
Gilgit
NORTHWEST
FRONTIER
KASHMIR
①
Murree
Kabul
Peshawar
Islamabad
Rawalpindi
Lahore
AFGHANISTAN
Faisalabad
PUNJAB
Multan
Bahawalpur
Quetta
Indus River
Jacobabad
Larkana
Sukkur
PAKISTAN
INDIA
BALUCHISTAN
SIND
IRAN
Rann of Kutch
Karachi
Mouths of the Indus
① Occupied by PAKISTAN but claimed by India
② Occupied by INDIA but claimed by Pakistan
ARABIAN SEA
0
400 Miles

him the background he needed to understand and strive for parliamentary democracy for Pakistan. Liaquat's efforts might have paved the way for democracy in Pakistan had he not been assassinated in October 1951.

The assassination of Liaquat opened the door to the succession of military leaders that followed. Ghulam Mohammad assumed the position of governor-general and formed an alliance of the military and the landed families of the Punjab. This alliance brought the power of the military to the fore and then weakened and eventually eliminated the powers of the prime minister. As these internal power struggles continued, the problems of a divided country grew. As early as the Second Constituent Congress in 1955, the issue of autonomy for East Pakistan was raised.

Ghulam Mohammad died in August 1955. He was succeeded by General Iskander Mirza, whose rule was marked by turmoil among the various factions within the country. Groups of Muslims argued over what role the religion of Islam should play in the governing of the new country. Mirza alienated the different regions by trying to force the country to become *One Unit,* as outlined in the 1956 constitution. In 1958 Mirza was forced to invoke martial law when the Khan of Kalat declared independence for Baluchistan, a province in the newly formed Pakistan. The already strained relations between East and West Pakistan were worsened by the assassination of Dr. Kahn Sahib, the chief minister of West Pakistan. On October 27, 1958, President Mirza was sent into exile in Britain by the leading generals of the army.

General Mohammad Ayub Khan became Pakistan's new leader. With the constitution suspended, Ayub was clearly a military dictator. However, he used his power to enact a series of reforms. The rule of Ayub Khan is marked by three basic areas of action. First, Ayub suppressed any possible opposition within or outside the government. Secondly, he put forth a number of reforms ranging from the Muslim Family Laws Ordinance which helped establish some basic rights for women, to major land reforms which put a limit on the amount of land one person could own. Thirdly, he instituted a program of *Basic Democracies* that were intended to introduce democracy gradually into the country.

It was Ayub's theory that the people could not be ruled democratically until they understood how democracy worked and how they could participate in it. His Basic Democracies program involved setting up a multitiered system starting with a *union council*. Each council, representing about ten thousand people, worked up to larger councils at higher levels. Ayub felt that the Basic Democracies program would educate the people in self-government. This would help create an arena in which the next generation of politicians could develop. Despite its overtly paternalistic approach, the Basic Democracies offered real hope for bringing democracy to Pakistan. The program was doomed almost from the beginning, however. Factionalism within Pakistan seemed stronger than even the most powerful dictator.

In 1965 Ayub found himself embroiled in a border war with India. The failure of the Ayub government to gain stated objectives in the dispute either militarily or at the bargaining table touched off domestic violence throughout Pakistan. In Lahore and Karachi, angry mobs burned the United States Information Service libraries. By February 1966 the opposition had become so intense that Ayub called for a national conference of political leaders to take place in Lahore. Of the seven hundred delegates present, only twenty-one were from East Pakistan, the more heavily populated part of the country.

The independence sentiments first voiced in 1954 by the East Pakistanis were becoming louder and better organized. The East Pakistani position, under the leadership of Sheikh Mujibur Rahman, kept the conference from proceeding on its stated goals of setting national objectives and issues. Because of the ineffectiveness of the congress to make any progress, among other reasons, Foreign Minister Zulfikar Ali Bhutto resigned and became a leader of the opposition. In late 1967, Bhutto formed a new political party, the Pakistan People's Party. By the early months of 1969, Ayub had lost control of the country. Mob rule was rampant, especially in East Pakistan. The situation was further complicated by Ayub becoming seriously ill. On March 25, 1969, General Agha Mohammad Yahya Khan assumed power and Ayub resigned.

On taking charge of the country, Yahya suspended the Constitution of 1962 and became the Chief Martial Law Administrator. In an attempt to hold the country together, Yahya promised elections. After several delays and postponements the first direct elections in the brief history of Pakistan took place. They were held on December 7, 1970 in most of the country and on January 17, 1971 in some parts of East Pakistan. The Awami League, representing the East Pakistani independence movement, won 167 out of 169 seats allotted to East Pakistan. Bhutto's Pakistan People's Party won a majority in West Pakistan.

Zulfikar Ali Bhutto

Zulfikar Ali Bhutto was born on January 5, 1928 into one of the rich and powerful landowning families of Sind province. His father, Sir Shah Nawaz Khan Bhutto, had been an active civil servant prior to the creation of Pakistan and had been knighted for his services to the British crown. Zulfikar Ali Bhutto's mother, Lady Khurshid, was from Bombay, India. Born a Hindu, she converted to Islam after her marriage. Sir Shah Nawaz served in many positions within the colonial administration of the subcontinent, primarily in Bombay. Sir Shah Nawaz was also one of the early advocates of the creation of a separate Muslim state on the subcontinent.

Zulfikar Ali Bhutto was raised in this politically active environment while experiencing all the benefits of belonging to one of the elite families of Sind. The Bhuttos can trace their lineage back to antiquity. For 350 years, the family has been based on its land in Sind province. They converted to Islam four hundred years ago and prior to that probably belonged to the aristocratic Rajput caste of Hindu warriors. Sir Shah Nawaz was the youngest son of his particular branch of the family, and the bulk of the land was ruled over by his older brother.

Sir Shah Nawaz was rather progressive and broke with the traditions of his class when he saw to it that his son, Zulfikar Ali Bhutto, received a modern education. Zulfikar Ali Bhutto was tutored at home until he was nine and was then sent to Cathedral Boys' School in Bombay, where the family was living at the time. On his first attempt at the Senior Cambridge Exam in December 1945, he failed to receive a passing grade. A year later, in December 1946, he passed his Cambridge Exam.

In the fall of 1947, Zulfikar Ali Bhutto enrolled at the University of Southern California and was the first Bhutto to go to school in the West. He transferred to the University of California at Berkeley in January 1949. At Berkeley he majored in political science and graduated with honors in 1950. From California he went to Oxford University in England, where he studied law. He received his Master of Arts in Jurisprudence in 1952 and went to Lincoln's Inn in London to prepare for his bar exams. He was called to the Bar in 1953 but returned to Pakistan where his father had taken ill and his first child awaited him.

In a tradition that was intended to keep the land held by the powerful families, children are often married at an early age to their cousins. Zulfikar Ali Bhutto was no exception. When he was twelve and his cousin Amir was eight, they were married. It was a marriage intended to help maintain the power of the Bhutto clan. After the marriage ceremony, Amir returned to live with her family. In 1951, while Zulfikar Ali Bhutto was home on vacation from Oxford, he met and fell in love with Nusrat Ispahani, the daughter of an Iranian businessman. Zulfikar Ali Bhutto broke with the tradition of marrying within the family and on September 8, 1951, Zulfikar Ali Bhutto and Nusrat were married. Islamic law allows a man to have as many as four wives. Zulfikar Ali Bhutto had asked for and received permission from his first wife, with whom he had never lived, to take a second wife.

Nusrat Bhutto came from a progressive urban family. She and her sisters had not been kept in seclusion, as were girls in many traditional Pakistani families. Nusrat Bhutto and her sisters had been educated and had attended college. They were allowed to drive their own cars and had even served in the National Guard, a paramilitary group made up of women. After marrying, Zulfikar Ali Bhutto and Nusrat Bhutto lived for a time in England. While pregnant, Nusrat Bhutto returned to Pakistan. She lived in seclusion, or purdah, with the other Bhutto women while her husband completed his studies in England.

The first of their four children, Benazir Bhutto, was born at Pinto Hospital in Karachi on June 21, 1953. Zulfikar Ali Bhutto did not meet his new daughter until he returned to Pakistan at the completion of his studies. Benazir Bhutto was three months old when her father finally got to see her.

Now back in Karachi for good, Zulfikar Ali Bhutto opened a law practice and assumed the management of the family lands. Due to his father's illness, the family estates had been neglected. Bhutto put himself to the task of getting things back on track while participating in the social life of Karachi. There is no doubt that he was a well-educated and capable young man, but his position near the top of Pakistani society also played a major part in launching his political career.

Like the British who had ruled them, the landed gentry of Pakistan has a passion for shooting. One of the best shooting preserves in Pakistan is located on the Bhutto family lands. During the first few years after Zulfikar Ali Bhutto returned to Pakistan, he could often be found on the weekends shooting with family and friends. Among the friends of his family who attended these shoots were then President Iskander Mirza and the head of the army, General Ayub Khan. Both men were apparently impressed with the young Berkeley- and Oxford-educated lawyer.

President Mirza was determined to utilize the talent of Zulfikar Ali Bhutto within the government. At first Zulfikar Ali Bhutto seemed to be caught up in the machinations of power as Mirza would nominate him for a position and first Prime Minister Choudhury Mohammad Ali and then later Prime Minister Hussain Shaheed Suhrawardy would turn him down.

In September 1957, Zulfikar Ali Bhutto was once again appointed to a position as a member of the United Nations delegation. This time no one objected, and Zulfikar Ali Bhutto, now twenty-nine, was on the road that would eventually lead him to the top of Pakistani politics—and ultimately to his death. At the United Nations, Zulfikar Ali Bhutto gave a speech entitled "The Definition of Aggression," which was well received. His tenure in New York was cut short when his father died. It took about two months for him to set his father's affairs straight. His next assignment was to attend the United Nations Conference on the Law of the Sea. He impressed people there as well.

On October 7, 1958, Iskander Mirza canceled elections and declared martial law. Just short of three weeks later, on October 27, 1958, General Ayub Khan staged a coup d'état. President Mirza was exiled, and General Ayub Khan assumed sole command of Pakistan. Although the military was now firmly in control of the country, Ayub wanted to include as many civilians as possible in his new government. Zulfikar Ali Bhutto's social position, talents, education, experience at the United Nations, and friendship with Ayub made him an obvious choice for inclusion in the government.

Zulfikar Ali Bhutto's first appointment under Ayub was as minister of commerce. At age thirty he became the youngest minister in Pakistan's brief history. In 1960, Zulfikar Ali Bhutto gave up his position as minister of commerce, and for the next two years he simultaneously ran four ministries. He became the minister of minority affairs; minister of national reconstruction and information; minister of fuel, power, and natural resources; and minister of Kashmir affairs. When General Ayub Khan instituted a new constitution and reformed his government in 1962, Zulfikar Ali Bhutto was the only original cabinet member to be included in the new government.

Throughout the four years he had served in the first Ayub cabinet, Zulfikar Ali Bhutto had been called on frequently to represent the government of Pakistan as a negotiator with and envoy to a number of foreign countries. He excelled in these situations, so it was not surprising that in the new government he was appointed minister of external affairs, a position comparable to the secretary of state in the United States. Over the next three years he was extremely active in Pakistan's foreign affairs, attending conferences and visiting foreign countries.

During this time, he is credited with reopening relations with Afghanistan, settling boundary disputes with the People's Republic of China, and enhancing Pakistan's image in the world community. When Ayub Khan began his second presidential term, Zulfikar Ali Bhutto retained his position as foreign minister. He was included in Ayub's inner circle as one of his four most trusted advisers.

Although Zulfikar Ali Bhutto was still a member of the right-wing Muslim League, the left-wing politics that he had displayed as a college student in California began to reappear. Ayub Khan was a staunch ally of the United States, while Zulfikar Ali Bhutto saw the U.S. as too domineering and unwilling to give Pakistan the military backing it needed in its struggle against India. Zulfikar Ali Bhutto saw the People's Republic of China, who had had its own conflicts with India, as Pakistan's natural ally.

Among other reasons, Zulfikar Ali Bhutto's position as a hard liner against India is part of what eventually caused his falling-out with Ayub Khan. In 1965 the ongoing tension between India and Pakistan once again flared into armed conflict. The undemarcated border between India and Pakistan in the Kashmir was the setting for an increasing number of skirmishes between the troops of both countries. A cease-fire was negotiated in the United Nations Security Council and President Ayub met with Indian Prime Minister Lal Bahadur Shastri at Tashkent in the Soviet Union. A mutual withdrawal of forces was agreed upon. The people of Pakistan were angry because they felt the war had accomplished nothing and had cost too many lives and too much money.

Demonstrations erupted in most of the urban areas of Pakistan. Politicians as well as students demonstrated. A national conference was called, but nothing was accomplished when the East Pakistanis used the conference to push for Bengali independence. Zulfikar Ali Bhutto was among those who saw the Tashkent agreement as a sign of weakness, and he tried to resign from the government. Ayub refused his resignation and, instead, waited until July when he sent Zulfikar Ali Bhutto on a forced sick leave to London and announced Bhutto's resignation.

Zulfikar Ali Bhutto became a vocal opponent of the government of President Ayub. By December 1967, Zulfikar Ali Bhutto had channeled his opposition into forming the Pakistan People's Party. Zulfikar Ali Bhutto's party grew rapidly and soon posed a threat to Ayub's government. On November 13, 1968, Ayub had Zulfikar Ali Bhutto arrested and sent to jail for allegedly causing violent antigovernment demonstrations. Zulfikar Ali Bhutto was released in February 1969. His time in jail enhanced his position as the opposition leader and gave him an aura of martyrdom that fueled his popularity.

The vocal and now often violent opposition to the Ayub government precipitated another coup. In March 1969 General Agha Mohammad Yahya Khan became the next military leader to head the country of Pakistan. Yahya suspended the constitution of 1962 and declared himself chief martial law administrator. Yahya and his generals were caught up in the irresistible forces that were destined to tear Pakistan apart.

As crisis approached, Yahya, in a nationwide broadcast on November 28, 1969, promised the country a new constitution and elections. These were set for October 5, 1970, but were held in December, after being postponed by Yahya. On December 7, 1970, and January 17, 1971, the first truly representative elections in Pakistan's history took place. In East Pakistan the Awami League, which led the inde-

Zulfikar Ali Bhutto rides through his home village of Larkana after being released in February 1969 from three months' imprisonment. His supporters may have saved his life when they grabbed a would-be assassin who aimed a pistol at him.

pendence movement, won 167 of the 169 East Pakistani seats in the new National Assembly, giving them a majority of the Assembly seats. In West Pakistan, Zulfikar Ali Bhutto and the Pakistan People's Party ran using the slogan *Islam our Faith, Democracy our Policy, and Socialism our Economy.* They won a majority of West Pakistani seats.

The peaceful transfer of power from the military to the newly elected National Assembly depended upon Yahya and the leaders of the two parties coming to terms. Holding a majority of the seats in the National Assembly, Sheik Mujib ur-Rahman (Mujib), the leader of the Awami League, wished to assert his right to form the new government. This was unacceptable to Zulfikar Ali Bhutto. When talks between Mujib, Yahya, and Zulfikar Ali Bhutto broke down, the Pakistan People's Party decided to boycott the National Assembly. On March 25, 1971, the crisis came to a head: Mujib declared independence for East Pakistan, and the country of Bangladesh was born.

The inability of Zulfikar Ali Bhutto, Yahya, and Mujib to reach a compromise can be seen as the direct catalyst to the civil war that followed. It could be argued that as the minority party in the new National Assembly, the Pakistan People's Party should have been the one to make concessions. It could be further argued that Zulfikar Ali Bhutto, by calling for the boycott of the National Assembly, should share the blame for the civil war.

The civil war between East and West Pakistan was devastating for both sides. Zulfikar Ali Bhutto, however, benefited. On December 20, 1971, he became president and chief martial law administrator of the reduced state of Pakistan. Although the problems of East versus West Pakistan were technically solved, Zulfikar Ali Bhutto still faced many of the same problems that the country had faced in 1947.

The most pressing problem was coming to terms with India and Bangladesh. Zulfikar Ali Bhutto traveled to Simla to meet with the Prime Minister of India, Indira Gandhi, on June 28, 1972. The Simla Agreement that came out of the meeting provided for the return of Pakistani prisoners and territory captured by India during the civil war. On the negative side Zulfikar Ali Bhutto had to concede to the dominance of India's position in Southwest Asia. He also agreed that Pakistan would not seek assistance from other countries in their problems with India and Bangladesh.

With the immediate problems of India and Bangladesh solved, Zulfikar Ali Bhutto then turned to restoring the country to constitutional rule. A new constitution was drawn up and put into effect on Pakistan Independence Day, August 14, 1973. The new constitution called for a parliamentary system with stipulations that made it almost impossible for the prime minister to be removed by the legislative branch. Despite the democratic reforms, Zulfikar Ali Bhutto ruled much as his predecessors had done. Although Zulfikar Ali Bhutto had the support of the military, his main source of power stemmed from his personal charisma and the popularity of the Pakistan People's Party.

Bhutto accomplished much in his five-and-a-half years as the leader of Pakistan. He worked to break the economic hold of the so-called "Twenty-two Families." He purged the military of over 1400 officers who he feared would support yet another military takeover of the country. He reformed the civil service and the functioning of the government bureaucracy.

Two events were to cause the downfall of Zulfikar Ali

Pakistani President Zulfikar Ali Bhutto (second from left) and Indian Prime Minister Indira Gandhi met in 1972. At left is Benazir Bhutto, who accompanied her father to India.

Bhutto. One was his appointment of General Zia ul-Haq as army chief of staff, and the other was the elections in March 1977. In response to the call for elections, nine opposition parties joined forces as the Pakistan National Alliance. The elections were hotly contested, and the Pakistan National Alliance seemed to be riding a wave of public support. However, when the election results were announced on March 7, 1977, the Pakistan People's Party had apparently won 154 seats, and the Pakistan National Alliance had won only 38. The Pakistan National Alliance challenged the election results and called for a new election. As Zulfikar Ali Bhutto had done before, the Pakistan National Alliance now refused to join the new government. After months of turmoil, the specter of the military once again raised its head.

On July 5, 1977, the military, led by Chief of Staff General Zia ul-Haq, intervened. The military arrested many political leaders, and Zia declared martial law. Zulfikar Ali Bhutto would spend the next two years in prison wasting away at the hands of his military captors. He was eventually tried and sentenced to death on charges that were never really proven. He was hanged in prison on April 4, 1979.

Benazir Bhutto: The Formative Years

Benazir Bhutto was born at Pinto Hospital in Karachi, Pakistan, on June 21, 1953. Her mother, the former Nusrat Ispahani, is the daughter of an Iranian businessman. Her father, Zulfikar Ali Bhutto, was a member of one of Pakistan's wealthiest landowning families, an Oxford educated lawyer, a cabinet minister and ultimately Prime Minister of Pakistan.

Benazir Bhutto was the first child of Zulfikar and Nusrat Bhutto. They had three other children: Mir Murtaza, a son, born in 1954; Sanam, a daughter, born in 1957; and Shah Nawaz, a son, born in 1958.

At birth, Benazir Bhutto's skin was rosy pink, which is unusual among the usually dark-complexioned Pakistanis. Her pink complexion at birth became the basis of her lifelong family nickname: *Pinkie.* Her given name Benazir means "without comparison." She was named after an aunt who had died while in her early teens. On the day of her birth, her paternal grandmother, Lady Khurshid Bhutto, gave one hundred rupees to a poor man she passed on the street. This is a custom intended to provide a blessing for the newly born child.

Benazir Bhutto's early childhood was spent primarily in Karachi where her father opened his law practice, and at Larkana at the seat of the family estates, Al-Murtaza. Benazir Bhutto grew up with all the trappings of wealth that her family's position near the top of Pakistani society could provide. Servants waited on the family, and one of Benazir Bhutto's first words was supposedly *ao*, which means enter. She said this to a servant who knocked on the door while she was being toilet-trained.

Although her mother sewed and embroidered dresses for her, as she got older her clothes were more likely to come from Saks Fifth Avenue, an expensive department store in New York City. She had an English governess who taught her western table manners and cared for her and her sister and brothers. English was the language most likely to be spoken by her family, although Persian (her mother's native language), Sindhi (the language of the Sind Province where the Bhutto estates are located), and Urdu (the official language of Pakistan) were also spoken in the Bhutto home.

Both of Benazir Bhutto's parents were Muslims. Zulfikar Ali Bhutto, the rest of the Bhutto family, and most Pakistanis belong to the Sunni branch of Islam. Nusrat Bhutto, like most Iranians, belongs to the Shiite sect. Benazir Bhutto was raised as and is today a Sunni Muslim. Her family, however, was much more progressive in their views than the majority of the people in Pakistan.

This progressive attitude led her parents to provide her

with the best education available. A shy but happy child, she started nursery school when she was three, attending the Lady Jenning's Nursery School in Karachi. At age five she was enrolled at the Convent of Jesus and Mary School, run by Irish Catholic nuns. They taught in English and reportedly made no attempt to convert their Muslim students to Catholicism. In addition to her school work, Benazir Bhutto received private tutoring at home in both academic and religious subjects. She had to learn Arabic as part of her religious obligations. The Quran, the Islamic holy book, must be read in Arabic by Muslims.

When Benazir Bhutto was four, her father received his first appointment as a member of Pakistan's delegation to the United Nations, so from that point on, Zulfikar and Nusrat Bhutto were often away from home. When Benazir was eight, she was given the responsibility of keeping the household money while her parents were away. In 1963, when she was ten and her sister Sanam was seven, their governess quit, and they were sent to boarding school.

A branch of the Convent of Jesus and Mary School in Karachi, the boarding school they attended was in Murree, in the northern part of Pakistan in the foothills of the Himalayan mountains; in earlier times it had been the site of a British colonial fort. It was also the location of the Bhutto's summer house. (The elevation in Murree made it a gathering spot for wealthy Pakistanis during the intense summer heat.) At boarding school Benazir Bhutto had to fend for herself. There were no servants, as there were at home, to make her bed or to do the other chores required of her at Murree. She did well under the tutelage of the nuns, although she found it hard to adjust to the strict rules.

Benazir Bhutto was still at Murree two years later when the 1965 Kashmir War broke out between India and Pakistan. Murree is not far from the area that was being fought over and directly on the logical invasion route that India might use. The nuns prepared the students for the possibility of attack, but fortunately the feared invasion never came.

In her early teens Benazir Bhutto returned to the Karachi branch of the Convent of Jesus and Mary school. In 1968, while she was preparing for her O-level exams, her father was arrested and put in Mianwali Prison, which was known for its horrible conditions. He was later transferred to Sahiwal Prison, where rats shared the cells.

Benazir Bhutto's life was not entirely dedicated to her studies. She and her friends also found time to go to the Sindh Club where they could swim, play squash, and socialize with other young people. Before her father's falling-out with General Ayub, Zulfikar Ali Bhutto would often see to it that Benazir and her siblings would get to meet the various foreign dignitaries visiting Pakistan. This provided her with an early introduction into one aspect of the workings of government.

The O-Level exams, which cover the last three years of secondary school, were held in December 1968. Due to the unrest in Pakistan at the time, the nuns at the Convent of Joseph and Mary made arrangements for the exams to be administered at the embassy of the Vatican. Benazir Bhutto also took the Scholastic Aptitude Test and an entrance exam for Radcliffe at about the same time. In April of 1969, she was accepted to Radcliffe College, a part of Harvard University in Cambridge, Massachusetts.

Benazir Bhutto at Radcliffe

When Benazir Bhutto arrived at Radcliffe in the fall of 1969, she was only sixteen—two years younger than most of her classmates. She was the first Bhutto woman to attend college in the West. Her mother accompanied her to the United States and stayed in Cambridge for two weeks helping her to get settled. Muslims are required to pray five times a day facing Mecca, their holy city, located in Saudi Arabia. Nusrat Bhutto ascertained Mecca's direction so that her daughter's prayers would be done properly.

Soon after her mother left to return to Pakistan, Benazir Bhutto decided that her traditional Pakistani attire, a shalwar khameez which is a tunic worn with pants, was not the most practical wardrobe for the climate and styles of Cambridge. A trip to the Harvard Coop in Harvard Square provided her with a wardrobe more appropriate for a coed of the time. The Harvard Coop fills the needs of the Harvard community and carries everything from books to toothbrushes and clothes to appliances. Jeans and sweatshirts were the uniform of this generation of college students, and like most college students, Benazir Bhutto seemed to want to fit in. Her hair was already straight, and she let it grow long. Many people pointed out to her that she looked remarkably like the popular folk singer Joan Baez.

In many ways Benazir Bhutto was an enigma to her college friends and acquaintances who came to know her by her family nickname, "Pinkie." On the one hand, she was a typical college student of the time, while on the other hand she continued to observe orthodox Islamic rules. She didn't smoke, drink, take drugs, or eat foods forbidden to Muslims. She did, however, develop a taste for ice cream cones and would often go with her friends to Brigham's in Harvard Square, where she liked to order peppermint stick ice cream with sprinkles. Until she arrived at Radcliffe, she had never answered her own phone or gone anywhere without the family chauffeur to take her. She adhered to some parts of the Muslim dress code by always wearing sweat pants when she played squash since Muslim traditions require women to cover their legs. She observed the Islamic taboo against dancing but would spend hours debating the problems of the world with her friends. She not only talked about the problems; she stood up for her beliefs as well.

Benazir Bhutto was a part of the anti-Vietnam War movement at Harvard. She marched against the Vietnam War on Boston Common and in Washington, D.C. She demonstrated despite the fact that she knew she could have been deported for doing so. Her opposition to the war must have been on political grounds because, when Pakistan fought its civil war in East Pakistan, she was a staunch defender of her country's right to use military force to try and stop the division of the country.

Benazir Bhutto also became interested in the women's movement. It is in part from this interest that she was much later able to see herself as the leader of a country, as a wife, and as a mother at the same time.

When one of her professors, Michael Walzer, criticized Pakistan and its military policies for its role in the civil war in East Pakistan, Benazir Bhutto stood up in class and refuted his statements. Her impassioned defense of her country was the first indication of what a moving and powerful public speaker she would become.

Benazir Bhutto had originally intended to study psychology at Radcliffe but eventually decided to seek a degree in comparative government. It was her plan at this time to enter the diplomatic corps of Pakistan after graduation. This desire was fueled by her father, who would often include her in his official visits to foreign countries when they coincided with her college vacations.

When Benazir Bhutto was a junior at Radcliffe, General Yahya Khan sent Zulfikar Ali Bhutto to the United Nations in New York. He was to try and negotiate a settlement to the Indian military intervention on behalf of the East Pakistani fight for independence. As soon as he learned he was on his way to New York, Zulfikar Ali Bhutto called his daughter and invited her to join him. With the idealism of a college student, Benazir Bhutto expected Pakistan to be vindicated and India to be condemned by the United Nations Security Council. The opposite outcome proved to be a bitter lesson in the politics of power.

For a variety of reasons that had nothing to do with what is just or unjust, the superpowers sided with India, and Bangladesh was created. Zulfikar Ali Bhutto had stormed out of the Security Council in anger, and his daughter had been right behind him. One ironic outcome of Benazir Bhutto's visit to the United Nations was that the woman who would eventually become the prime minister of Pakistan met the man who would later be the president of the United States. George Bush was President Nixon's ambassador to the United Nations and, while visiting Zulfikar Ali Bhutto, was introduced to Benazir Bhutto. Bush remarked at the time that one of his sons was at Harvard with Benazir Bhutto and suggested that, if she needed any assistance, she should look him up.

Zulfikar Ali Bhutto speaks to the United Nations General Assembly.

When her father returned to Pakistan, he was to become the head of the country. As the leader of the largest political party in Pakistan, he was probably the only civilian with sufficient experience in government and enough popular support to lead Pakistan out of its defeat by India and its loss of Bangladesh. On December 20, 1971, Zulfikar Ali Bhutto became president and chief martial law administrator of Pakistan.

As the leader of his country, he continued to include Benazir Bhutto whenever he could, taking her on visits to foreign countries and discussing policy with her. Consciously or unconsciously, he was preparing her to follow in his footsteps.

His first order of business as head of the government was to reach a settlement with India. On June 28, 1972, Benazir Bhutto accompanied her father to Simla, India, where Zulfikar Ali Bhutto and Indian Prime Minister Indira Gandhi met behind closed doors to try and settle their problems. Due in part to the secrecy of their talks, the eye of the media was turned on Benazir Bhutto. She experienced the scrutiny that would continue as she became more and more important in the politics of her country.

While at Radcliffe, Benazir Bhutto also accompanied her father to China and sat in on his meetings with Chairman Mao, which made her liberal, intellectual friends at Harvard green with envy. Benazir Bhutto also visited the Nixon White House when her father was in Washington, D.C., on a state visit.

Benazir Bhutto seemed capable of fitting in wherever she went. She was fond of attending the many athletic events at Harvard. On her frequent visits to the home of Professor John Kenneth Galbraith, the former American ambassador to India, she seemed more like the young woman who would one day lead her country. When she met with other Pakistanis who were part of the Cambridge academic community, she would revert to her traditional clothing and once more seem the aristocrat that she is.

In 1973, Benazir Bhutto graduated cum laude from Radcliffe, which has since been absorbed by Harvard University. She had learned and experienced much in her four years at Harvard in the turbulent early seventies. Despite the changes she may have gone through, two things remained steadfast: her devotion to Islam and her devotion to Pakistan. The two are intertwined in this woman who was destined for leadership. Pakistan exists as a homeland for the Muslims on the subcontinent, and Benazir Bhutto represents the first generation to be born Pakistani.

Benazir Bhutto at Oxford

Benazir Bhutto entered Lady Margaret Hall at Oxford College in the fall of 1973. Unlike the meek child who had entered Radcliffe four years before, Benazir Bhutto went to Oxford as the daughter of the prime minister of Pakistan and a self-confident young woman. The people of England are generally more aware of the goings-on in their former colonies than the people in the United States. This made Benazir Bhutto more of a celebrity than she had ever been at Radcliffe. Great Britain, with its tenacious continuance of the monarchy, is much more class-conscious than the United States. At Oxford, Benazir Bhutto was more likely to be found among those who were her social and economic equals.

There were no more walks through Harvard Square to go to Brigham's for ice cream. At Oxford she would race

At Oxford, Benazir was elected to the prestigious position of president of the Oxford Union. She was only the third woman to hold that post.

off to the newly opened Baskin Robbins in London in the yellow MG convertible that her father had given her. And at Oxford her enjoyment of debating took on a more formalized air as she joined the Oxford Union.

The Oxford Union Debating Society, which was formed in 1823 and is modeled on the British House of Commons, is said to be a training ground for future politicians. Benazir Bhutto joined at her father's request but soon found the Union to her liking. During the many debates she participated in, her powers of oratory, which had only begun to emerge at Radcliffe, blossomed. She also became active in the running of the union. She served on its standing committee and as treasurer. Her first attempt to become president of the Oxford Union Debating Society ended in defeat.

After three years at Oxford she had completed her second Bachelor of Arts degree in philosophy, politics, and economics. She then decided to stay on for another year to study international law and diplomacy and to make another run for the presidency of the union. Her brother, Mir Murtaza Bhutto, joined her at Oxford during her fourth year. In December 1976, after a very energetic campaign, Benazir Bhutto was elected president of the Oxford Union. She served a three-month term which began in January 1977—the first Asian woman to serve as president. Her father had been the first Asian person to hold that office. It is ironic that it would be eleven years before Benazir Bhutto would run for another elected office and that her second political victory would make her prime minister of one hundred million Pakistanis.

Right after graduation, fresh from her success as president of the union, Benazir Bhutto returned to Pakistan to take a job in the office of her father, the prime minister.

Return to Pakistan

Early in 1977, while Benazir Bhutto was serving her term as president of the Oxford Union Debating Society, her father was facing growing unrest in Pakistan. Some believe that Zulfikar Ali Bhutto's pro–People's Republic of China stance and his commitment to developing nuclear weapons for Pakistan caused the United States to assist in the destabilization of the Bhutto government. Others believe that it was Zulfikar Ali Bhutto's repressive action toward his political opponents that was the catalyst for the unrest.

To appease the opposition, elections were called for March 1977. During the election campaign, the nine-party coalition called the Pakistan National Alliance seemed to be giving the Pakistan People's Party a run for their money. Thus when the Pakistan People's Party won 154 of 200 seats in Parliament, there was an immediate outcry from the opposition parties that the election had been rigged. Using a technique pioneered by Zulfikar Ali Bhutto, they protested the election by refusing to participate in the new government. Conditions went from bad to worse, with violent demonstrations against the Bhutto government.

On her return home in early June, Benazir Bhutto had moved into an office next to her father's. She was in the process of reviewing many of his papers when her father was trying to negotiate a settlement with the opposition leaders. As negotiations continued, Benazir Bhutto, her sister, and two brothers met with their parents in Rawalpindi on June 25, 1977. No one in the family knew that this would be the last time they would all be together.

In early July 1977, it looked like a settlement was about to be reached between Bhutto and his adversaries. However, the man that Zulfikar Ali Bhutto had promoted to head the military, General Zia ul-Haq, seized power in a bloodless coup on July 5, 1977. General Zia declared himself chief martial law administrator, promised new elections in ninety days, and arrested his boss, Zulfikar Ali Bhutto. General Zia had Zulfikar Ali Bhutto taken to the family summer house in Murree, where he was kept under house arrest for three weeks.

When Zulfikar Ali Bhutto was released by the military, he began campaigning for the promised October elections. Although there is evidence of some irregularities in the March elections, it is most likely that the Pakistan People's Party would still have had a clear majority. Zulfikar Ali Bhutto's popularity among the people of Pakistan was obviously a clear threat to General Zia.

On September 3, 1977, Zulfikar Ali Bhutto was arrested again and charged with conspiracy to murder at least one of his political opponents. Ten days later, he was out on bail. He returned to the family estate, Al-Murtaza, near Larkana. On September 17, the house was stormed by seventy army and police commandos, and Zulfikar Ali Bhutto was arrested for what would be the last time. General Zia also had thousands of other members of the Pakistan People's Party arrested.

With Zulfikar Ali Bhutto in jail, it fell to Benazir Bhutto and her mother to keep the campaign going. Benazir Bhutto made her first speech in Faisalabad. Her experiences in college and especially at the Oxford Union, coupled with her burning desire to see her father vindicated, made her a riveting speaker. It was quickly apparent to General Zia that Benazir Bhutto could become a real threat. After her third speech, on September 29, 1977, she was arrested. The house she was staying in was declared a subjail, and Benazir Bhutto was held under house arrest for fifteen days. The day after her arrest, September 30, 1977, General Zia called off the promised elections and intensified his reign of terror.

General Zia instituted public floggings and jailed thousands of people who were opposed to his military takeover. General Zia had the support of the most conservative among the religious community. Throughout his reign, Zia pushed his country toward Islamic fundamentalism—which eroded the civil rights of the people, especially women.

As fall approached, Benazir Bhutto's sister, Sanam, returned to Harvard, her brother Shah Nawaz returned to school in Switzerland, and her brother Mir Murtaza left for England. Benazir Bhutto and her mother were left with the responsibility of directing the defense of Zulfikar Ali Bhutto and trying to keep the Pakistan People's Party active. Considering their wealth, it would have been easy for Benazir Bhutto and her mother to leave the country and live comfortably. It is a credit to her dedication to her father and to her sense of justice that she stayed, realizing that she could easily become one of General Zia's victims.

Zulfikar Ali Bhutto is not blameless. As the prime minister of Pakistan, he used his position to subdue his political adversaries. He came to power as the appointee of a military regime, and his power came to an end at the hands of the next military regime. The charges that were brought against him in September 1977, however, were trumped up by the Zia regime and based on tainted confessions of tortured prisoners. There was little if anything in the way of factual evidence. Possibly because of the absurdity of the charges, Benazir Bhutto was confident that her father would be acquitted.

Despite the abuses of power and other criticisms of Zulfikar Ali Bhutto, he had worked hard to enfranchise the people of Pakistan into the political process. He especially wanted to help those at the bottom of Pakistani society. Many of these people remained loyal to him and the Pakistan People's Party. With Zulfikar Ali Bhutto seeming more and more the martyr with each passing day, it was easy for these people to transfer their allegiance to his wife, Nusrat Bhutto, and increasingly to his daughter Benazir Bhutto.

On October 24, 1977, Zulfikar Ali Bhutto's trial began. He and four codefendants were charged with conspiracy to murder Ahmed Raza Kasuri, a political opponent. In 1974, Kasuri's car had been attacked and fired upon. Kasuri survived the attack, but his father was killed. Kasuri claimed that Zulfikar Ali Bhutto was responsible for the attack. The normal legal process was altered, and the trial was moved from the usual lower court to the High Court of Lahore. The judge, recently appointed to the High Court by General Zia, was an old enemy of Zulfikar Ali Bhutto. The trial lasted for five months, and either Benazir Bhutto or her mother, and often both, tried to be there every day. In an effort to humiliate Zulfikar Ali Bhutto, he was forced to sit surrounded by security police in a special dock built just for this case.

After sitting through the five months of the trial, Benazir Bhutto was convinced that her father had won the case. Her father, however, understood that the trial was only a shallow attempt to make his eventual execution look legitimate.

In addition to the attempted murder/conspiracy charges against him, the Zia regime accused Zulfikar Ali Bhutto of a variety of other offenses, including misappropriation of funds and corruption. During this time, Benazir Bhutto pored over her father's personal papers and records, where she found the evidence needed to refute the ever-growing number of charges. The Zia-controlled newspapers would always print the charges but would not print the denials and the evidence that Benazir Bhutto found.

Benazir Bhutto and the members of the Pakistan People's Party who were still free made copies of the evidence which would clear Zulfikar Ali Bhutto of the government's charges and distributed them among the people. They also put out a pamphlet that presented the rumors and charges generated by Zia's people. They then told their version and presented the evidence that exposed the lies being spread about Zulfikar Ali Bhutto.

Throughout Zia's reign, the abuses of human rights were frequent and well documented. Public floggings and secret tortures were regular occurrences. Beatings, cigarette burns, and electric shock to the genitals were standard operating procedure in the jails of General Zia ul-Haq. Public executions were instituted. Under martial law General Zia made political activities of all kinds illegal and punishable by public flogging. Under Islamic law General Zia made it possible for people to lose a hand for stealing or be stoned to death for adultery.

Fortunately, Amnesty International, an international nonprofit organization which investigates and publicizes human rights violations around the world, never found evidence that these two punishments were used. Nusrat Bhutto tried, through her lawyers, to get the Supreme Court of Pakistan to declare the military takeover unconstitutional. The Supreme Court sided with Zia and declared martial law a necessity to maintain order in the country.

On December 16, 1977, the police stormed a cricket match that Benazir Bhutto and her mother were attending. The crowd was tear-gassed, and Nusrat Bhutto received a wound to the head that required twelve stitches. That evening Benazir Bhutto was arrested for the second time, and her mother was arrested while in the hospital. The implications of these arrests were far-reaching. General Zia was sending them a message that he would persecute them, as well as Zulfikar Ali Bhutto, if he needed to. Even more alarming to Muslim tradition was this attack against women. As Zulfikar Ali Bhutto's trial continued, the persecution of Nusrat and Benazir Bhutto escalated. They were both constantly under house arrest or externed, prohibited from going to or staying in one place or another. Often they were arrested and held just long enough to ensure that they missed their scheduled visits with Zulfikar Ali Bhutto, who was now in solitary confinement.

As the time for the court's decision approached, it seemed obvious that General Zia already knew the verdict. The army arrested and detained tens of thousands of Pakistan People's Party supporters. Frequently, the army was forced to use sports arenas and other large facilities to hold the ever-growing number of prisoners. Public floggings increased in number, and the police were arresting and flogging anyone who publicly said "Long live Bhutto."

On March 18, 1978, the Lahore high court unanimously handed down the expected guilty verdict and sentenced Zulfikar Ali Bhutto and his four codefendants to death by hanging. Appeals for clemency flooded into Pakistan from around the world. The leaders of the Soviet Union, China, Great Britain, Canada, France, Saudi Arabia, and other countries called upon General Zia to spare the life of Zulfikar Ali Bhutto. United States Senators George McGovern and Daniel Patrick Moynihan spoke on Bhutto's behalf in the United States Senate. Turkey offered asylum for Zulfikar Ali Bhutto. Resigned to his fate, Bhutto was willing to wait for his death, at peace with himself. He saw no point in being the further victim of the Zia kangaroo courts. His wife and daughter Benazir still wanted to fight the decision and on his behalf appealed the Lahore high court decision to the Supreme Court of Pakistan.

Ramsey Clark, former attorney general of the United States, attended the trial of Zulfikar Ali Bhutto as a private observer. He would later write in an article for *The Nation* that Zulfikar Ali Bhutto had not been allowed to speak in his own defense and that the evidence presented had not supported the guilty verdict. Legal experts claimed that there were many irregularities in the trial ranging from using hearsay evidence to torturing and bribing the witnesses. They also found that the court based its decision on testimony that conflicted with the physical evidence in the case.

During the time before and during the appeal, Benazir

Bhutto was constantly harassed by the military and the police. She was followed by convoys of police vehicles everywhere she went and was frequently in one state of detention or another. Sometimes she would be held prisoner in her own house. Other times the police and military would force her to leave one place to be locked up in another. When she was permitted to see her father, she was forced to visit him in the squalid cell where he was being kept.

Zulfikar Ali Bhutto was literally wasting away in jail. His body was covered with mosquito bites because the guards had removed the screens from his windows. He was underfed and had lost a great deal of weight. The guards at one point had put him in a cell next to a group detention cell that held fifteen insane men who yelled all night, preventing him from getting any sleep.

Benazir Bhutto worked hard during her father's appeal. She spent her time assisting the lawyers in transcribing the notes her father wrote in his prison cell. The lawyers had set up offices at Flashman's Hotel in Rawalpindi, the city where the supreme court sits. As they prepared their appeal, the hotel was frequently surrounded by the police and the military. The phones were tapped, and the various people working on behalf of Zulfikar Ali Bhutto were harassed and, on occasion, arrested. The courts had granted Benazir Bhutto the right to visit her father once every two weeks. Sometimes the authorities wouldn't come to get her, other times they would wait until late in the day so that she would only have time for a very short visit.

In September 1978, Benazir Bhutto was sent by her father on a tour of the Northwest Frontier Province and the Punjab to help bolster support for the Pakistan People's Party. During this same time, she also had to assume the duties as head of the family. With both her mother and father in jail and her two brothers in exile, she had to go to Larkana for a Muslim holiday and pray at the graves of the family ancestors. She also had to sit in judgment over a dispute between two of the tenants on the family estates. On October 4, 1978, she was arrested again.

As her father's appeal came to a conclusion in December 1978, Benazir Bhutto was held in detention and not allowed to attend. On December 18, 1978, Zulfikar Ali Bhutto was allowed to speak in his own defense. Hundreds of people packed the small courtroom as the now emaciated former prime minister made his final appeal for justice and his last public appearance. He spoke to the court for four days. By December 23, 1978, the trial was completed.

On February 6, 1979, the Supreme Court of Pakistan—in a four-to-three decision—denied the appeal and upheld the death sentence of the lower court. The four judges who voted against Zulfikar Ali Bhutto were all from the Punjab, the home province of General Zia, who again must have known the verdict in advance as he had members of the Pakistan People's Party arrested two days before the verdict was announced. During this time, Benazir Bhutto and her mother were denied permission to visit Zulfikar Ali Bhutto. Their only consolation was that mother and daughter were both being held at a police training camp in Sihala, near Rawalpindi. Zulfikar Ali Bhutto was still in the Rawalpindi District Jail nearby.

The world community spoke with almost one voice in their requests for clemency for Zulfikar Ali Bhutto. United States President Jimmy Carter, who had remained silent after the original verdict, now added his voice to the cries for a commutation of the death sentence of Zulfikar Ali Bhutto. Even Indira Gandhi, the former prime minister of India who had been a longtime adversary of Pakistan, worked on behalf of Zulfikar Ali Bhutto, writing letters to world leaders on Bhutto's behalf. It all fell on deaf ears. Even the risk that Zulfikar Ali Bhutto's death would cause him to become a martyr, rallying the Pakistan People's Party and others who opposed the military regime of General Zia, was not enough to stay the executioner's hand.

Every attempt by the lawyers had failed. On March 24, 1979, even the Supreme Court that had upheld his conviction requested that General Zia commute the sentence to life in prison. On April 3, 1979, Benazir Bhutto and her mother were rushed by limousine, escorted by two carloads of police, to Rawalpindi District Jail for an unscheduled three-hour visit with Zulfikar Ali Bhutto. It was clear to all that this would be their final meeting. The guards refused to open the door to the cell so that Benazir Bhutto and her mother were forced to say their final good-byes through the bars. The condition of Zulfikar Ali Bhutto at this point was so poor that death was not far away even if the regime had decided not to execute him.

Zulfikar Ali Bhutto was hanged at the Rawalpindi District jail sometime around 2:00 A.M. April 4, 1979. The usual time for executions was 6:00 A.M., but General Zia wanted to get Zulfikar Ali Bhutto buried before anyone knew he was dead. His body was spirited out of the city and flown to Larkana, 200 miles away, where the military had instituted a complete curfew. Zulfikar Ali Bhutto was buried in his ancestral graveyard, and no one from the family or the community was allowed to attend the hasty funeral.

News of Zulfikar Ali Bhutto's execution triggered protests and violence throughout Pakistan, even though General Zia had had the police round up over two thousand Pakistan People's Party leaders before the execution. Mass prayer meetings broke out into clashes with the police and military, who used clubs and tear gas to break up the demonstrations. The police arrested hundreds of demonstrators in an attempt to quiet the public outrage.

Time of Mourning

When Benazir Bhutto returned to Pakistan in 1977 after spending eight years studying, first in the United States and then in England, it was her intention to find a job in the foreign service of Pakistan. She would have been able to put her education in politics and government to practical use. Instead, she returned to Pakistan and witnessed her father's overthrow by a military coup. Then she had to live through the next year and a half of her father's persecution and imprisonment, which ended with his execution on April 4, 1979. Benazir Bhutto had worked in any way she could to help her father's defense. She had been his stand-in at political rallies and had researched his personal files to aid in his defense. In addition, Benazir Bhutto experienced the frustration and fear of imprisonment and harassment at the hands of the Zia government.

It would not have surprised anyone had Benazir Bhutto and her mother retired quietly, taking advantage of the wealth and comfort to which their position as members of the Pakistani aristocracy entitled them. Seven weeks after the death of Zulfikar Ali Bhutto, Benazir Bhutto and her mother were finally released from Sihala, where they had been held since February 1979. They could easily have retreated to their private estates and most likely would have been left alone by General Zia and his security forces. But they did not retreat. Nusrat Bhutto was in Iddat, which is the traditional period of mourning for a Muslim widow, which lasts four months and ten days. Benazir Bhutto became the figurehead of the Pakistan People's Party. She worked toward the expected victory of the party in the local elections in September and the scheduled national elections in November. At the time it seemed as though General Zia was sticking to his promise of a return to democracy.

In addition to assuming a leadership role with the Pakistan People's Party, Benazir Bhutto also had to continue in her role as head of the family. With her father dead, her two brothers in exile, and her mother in mourning, Benazir Bhutto returned to Al-Murtaza, the seat of the family estates. She needed to review the books and accounts of the family lands. The farms had been functioning under the direction of the various managers that the Bhuttos employed and had not been checked on since before General Zia overthrew her father almost two years before. It was at this time that Benazir Bhutto was forced to overcome the traditions of her country and to fill the leadership void of both the family and the Pakistan People's Party. Both of these tasks were considered men's jobs by Pakistani society. Yet, as the daughter of Zulfikar Ali Bhutto, Benazir Bhutto was accepted in these traditionally male roles.

The September local elections demonstrated the renewed appeal of the Pakistan People's Party. They showed that Zulfikar Ali Bhutto was an even bigger threat to the

General Zia continued to persecute Benazir Bhutto and her mother. He realized that they may have been even more of a threat to his government now that Zulfikar Ali Bhutto had been martyred.

Zia regime now that he had become a martyr of the people. The Pakistan People's Party swept the September elections and had high expectations for the November national elections. However, General Zia must have felt the reality of the threat that general elections posed for his regime. General Zia added new rules to the election process that were intended to make it more difficult for Benazir Bhutto and the Pakistan People's Party. At first the Pakistan People's Party thought of boycotting the elections. When they decided to go ahead and try and win the elections in spite of General Zia's manipulation of the electoral process, General Zia canceled the national elections.

On October 16, 1979, the day the elections were canceled, General Zia sent soldiers to the Bhutto home in Karachi and had Benazir Bhutto and her mother arrested. They were taken at gunpoint to Al-Murtaza, the ancestral home of the Bhuttos in Sind Province. They were held at Al-Murtaza for six months. General Zia outlawed political parties and decreed that anyone who belonged to a political party could be imprisoned for up to fourteen years.

As the first anniversary of Zulfikar Ali Bhutto's death approached, Benazir Bhutto and her mother petitioned the government for permission to visit his grave. Permission was denied, and General Zia's forces attempted to close the entire area around the Bhutto family graveyard. People attempting to visit the grave of the now martyred leader were harassed and arrested by the police. General Zia, in the face of mounting opposition, began to crack down on anyone who criticized him.

The Movement to Restore Democracy

General Zia, after three years in power, found himself in a precarious position. The Pakistan National Alliance, the party that had been instrumental in the downfall of Zulfikar Ali Bhutto, had become disillusioned with the military regime. Many Pakistan National Alliance members who had accepted positions within the Zia government were now leaving in protest or were being forced out by Zia. The Zia government had become, in many ways, a puppet of the United States. The invasion of Afghanistan by Soviet troops made Pakistan strategically important to the United States. President Ronald Reagan wanted to support the rebels fighting against the Soviet troops in Afghanistan. President Reagan needed the Zia government to be a conduit for military aid for the mujahedin, the Afghan freedom fighters. The United States has often given tacit approval to the erosion of human rights in countries that were strategically important in stemming communist imperialism. The United States Congress voted to approve a $3.2 billion, six-year aid package for General Zia and Pakistan. They also approved the sale of forty F–16 fighter planes for $1.1 billion in cash.

General Zia reportedly used some of the profits from his dealing with the United States to solidify his position within Pakistan. Purportedly, members of opposition political parties were offered money to join parties loyal to General Zia. Some claim that General Zia even tried to buy out top members of the Pakistan People's Party with offers of positions within his government. The level of corruption increased markedly during the Zia years. The Zia government is said to have diverted up to two-thirds of the relief money that was pouring in to aid the Afghan refugees who were flooding over the border into Pakistan. General Zia's attempts to buy out the opposition, coupled with the erosion of human rights, seemed only to galvanize the opposition against him.

In the fall of 1980, the Pakistan National Alliance—the party that had ultimately brought about the death of Zulfikar Ali Bhutto at the hands of General Zia—approached the Pakistan People's Party in hopes of forming an alliance. Benazir Bhutto was outraged that her father's friends and allies would even consider negotiating with the Pakistan National Alliance. She saw them as political opportunists who had cashed in on her father's downfall and death and who now wanted an alliance only because Zia was pushing them out.

Her mother, Nusrat Bhutto, looked at the offer of alliance more practically. She and other members of the Pakistan People's Party saw the alliance as a political necessity. They could not topple Zia on their own. It would take a ground swell of public pressure and possibly violence to unseat General Zia and his martial law government. In October 1980 a meeting was held at 70 Clifton, the Bhuttos' home in Karachi, with the Pakistan National Alliance and other political parties. Over the next five months an agreement was worked out between the Pakistan People's Party, the Pakistan National Alliance, and eight other parties.

Benazir Bhutto, despite her opposition to dealing with her father's enemies, realized the need for such an alliance and reluctantly supported it. On February 6, 1981, the leaders of the various parties signed a charter and the Movement to Restore Democracy was created. The announcement set off demonstrations and violence against the Zia government in Karachi and Quetta in the western part of Pakistan. At Karachi University, a student leader who had supported Zia was killed, and twelve of his followers were injured in a bombing. Earlier in the week he had been involved in a fight with students who supported the Bhuttos and the Pakistan People's Party.

The newly formed Movement to Restore Democracy scheduled a meeting for February 27, 1981, and General Zia responded on February 21, 1981, by arresting eighty-seven of the leaders of the group. Among those arrested was Nusrat Bhutto. She was held at Karachi Central Jail. This was the first time, despite all her other arrests, that Zia had put Nusrat Bhutto in a prison cell. Again, General Zia's attempts to stifle the opposition set off violent protests throughout the country. This time, however, some within the opposition tried a new tactic.

On March 2, 1981, a Pakistan International Airlines jet was hijacked while on a domestic flight in Pakistan and ordered to fly to Kabul, Afghanistan. In the week following the hijacking, thousands of people were arrested. On March 7, 1981, the police once again stormed 70 Clifton and arrested Benazir Bhutto. She was taken to Karachi Central Jail and held incommunicado for five days while the drama of the hijacking unfolded.

Al-Zulfikar was a secret Pakistan terrorist organization whose goal was to bring an end to the rule of General Zia. Also called the Pakistan Liberation Army, Al-Zulfikar was headed by Mir Murtaza Bhutto and Shah Nawaz Bhutto, Benazir Bhutto's brothers. They had left Pakistan shortly after General Zia had taken over and had not been back since. The hijacking of the Pakistan International Airlines flight was done by members of Al-Zulfikar. First, they had the plane flown to Kabul, Afghanistan, and then to Damascus, Syria, where thirteen days later the fifty-four passengers and crew members were released. While the plane was still in Kabul, the hijackers shot and killed a Pakistani diplomat, Tariq Rahim, who had been a military aide-de-camp to Prime Minister Zulfikar Ali Bhutto.

The objective of the hijackers was the release of political prisoners that were being held in Pakistan. Ultimately, fifty-five prisoners were released and sent to Syria. However, the ramifications of the hijacking within Pakistan were devastating to the Pakistan People's Party as well as to Benazir and Nusrat Bhutto. Neither of the Bhutto women had seen Mir Murtaza or Shah Nawaz Bhutto since they had left Pakistan, nor were the women in any way a part of the terrorist organization. General Zia, however, saw this as an opportunity to discredit Benazir Bhutto and her mother. Following their arrests in March, the Zia regime systematically arrested and tortured the top echelon of the Pakistan People's Party members in an attempt to create evidence that Benazir Bhutto and her mother were part of Al-Zulfikar.

The tactics that were used by Zia's agents were documented by Amnesty International. According to this source, people were beaten and starved; they were also held in dark cells so small that they couldn't lie down and in cells exposed to the searing heat of the desert sun. These and other techniques show the level of desperation that the Zia government felt in their attempt to discredit the Bhuttos. In some cases, when the police could not find the person they were after, they would arrest and torture other members of the person's family. Sometimes they would arrest the suspect's wife or a child who was not a part of the political movement. During this time, Benazir Bhutto was in solitary confinement in Sukkur Prison and her mother was being held incommunicado at Karachi Central Jail.

General Zia was apparently trying to build the same sort of flimsy case against Benazir and Nusrat Bhutto that he had built against Zulfikar Ali Bhutto. It speaks highly of the integrity of the members of the Pakistan People's Party and their loyalty to the Bhuttos that the government was never able to conjure up any evidence despite the extremes they went to. No doubt Mir Murtaza and Shah Nawaz Bhutto felt that Al-Zulfikar was the only way that they could fight back against the man who was responsible for their father's death. Unfortunately, among those who suffered the most by their actions were their mother and sister and those who remained loyal to them. Many believe that General Zia would have continued to persecute the Bhutto women anyway. Yet the actions of Al-Zulfikar gave him all the excuse he needed to intensify and broaden his attack on the opposition within Pakistan.

Benazir Bhutto was arrested on March 8, 1981, and after five days in Karachi Central Jail, she was put in solitary confinement in Sukkur Jail. According to Amnesty International, Benazir Bhutto and her mother were among six thousand people arrested in Pakistan in March of 1981 for political reasons. In Sukkur she was cut off from her family and from news of the outside. Her only contact with the events transpiring in Pakistan was from an occasional newspaper or magazine that was smuggled in to her by a sympathetic guard. Her ear infection, which had first begun bothering her during her father's trial over two years ago, flared up again. In addition, she developed other medical problems due to the squalid conditions in the prison.

Benazir Bhutto despaired over being detained in solitary confinement for so long. During her earlier arrests, the police or military had held her in one of her family's houses or in someone else's home. The solitary confinement caused her to become unable to eat, and she began to show the symptoms of anorexia. The doctors who examined her in prison also claimed that she had developed gynecological problems as well. In mid-April she was told that she had uterine cancer and that she was to be taken to Karachi to be operated on. Whether she had cancer or not has never been substantiated, and some believe that the Zia regime had planned to have her die on the operating table.

Her sister, Sanam, was able to see Benazir Bhutto in a

hospital ward briefly after her operation. Shortly after the operation—and against the directions of the doctors—Benazir Bhutto was moved first to Karachi Central Jail and then back to her cell at Sukkur Prison.

According to her original detention order, Benazir Bhutto was scheduled to be released on June 12, 1981. As she recovered from her mysterious operation, Benazir Bhutto developed a regimen for combating the long, tedious hours of solitary confinement. She began to force herself to eat and tried to exercise regularly. June 12 arrived, and along with it came a new detention order extending her confinement until September 12, 1981. Her sister was allowed to visit her on her birthday, June 21. It is ironic that the Zia regime employed the same tactics on this birthday as they had when Benazir Bhutto had planned to visit her father in prison on June 21, 1978. Sanam Bhutto was delayed again and again as she made the trip from Karachi to Sukkur Prison so that, once she finally arrived, she was able to visit for only a short time.

During the summer, Benazir Bhutto began to hear all sorts of strange noises in the night. Her guard told her that it was a ghost. Although very superstitious, Benazir Bhutto assumed that it was a ploy by her captors to try and increase the mental strain of solitary confinement. Despite the deprivations of Sukkur Prison, she never gave in to the offers of clemency in exchange for agreeing to stay out of politics.

In August 1981, Benazir Bhutto was moved from Sukkur Prison. In a perverse example of the cruelty of the Zia jailers, Benazir Bhutto was now incarcerated in the same cell that her mother had just been released from in the

Karachi Central Jail. As the date of the end of her current detention order approached, Benazir Bhutto allowed herself to hope that she would be permitted to leave jail.

In early September 1981, she was granted permission to attend the wedding of her sister, Sanam. For two days, Benazir Bhutto stayed awake constantly to visit with her family and the wedding guests. Relatives and friends came from all over the world to attend the wedding, and the joyous occasion renewed the sagging spirits of Benazir Bhutto. Many of the guests found it hard to believe when the next day a convoy of police arrived to return Benazir Bhutto to her cell in Karachi Central Jail. At this time she learned through her lawyers that she would remain a prisoner until she agreed to refrain from all political activities.

While she was attending her sister's wedding, she also learned that her friend from Harvard, Peter Galbraith, had been in Pakistan as a representative of the United States Senate Foreign Relations Committee. While in Pakistan he had tried to see Benazir Bhutto in jail. He had been unable to gain permission for a visit. He returned to Washington where he brought Benazir Bhutto's plight to the attention of Senators Claiborne Pell and Charles Percy and other members of the committee. As a result of his efforts and the reports of human rights violations within Pakistan that Amnesty International had published, Senator Pell was able to attach an amendment to the Pakistan Aid Bill. The amendment called for the restoration of democracy in Pakistan. As Benazir Bhutto returned to her cell in Karachi Central Jail, she was hopeful that she would soon be free.

On September 25, 1981, Chaudhry Zahur Elahi, a minister in the Zia government who had accepted as a gift

General Zia's pen after Zia signed Zulfikar Ali Bhutto's death warrant, was assassinated. Maulvi Mushtaq Hussein, the former chief justice of the Lahore high court who had originally sentenced Zulfikar Ali Bhutto to death, was wounded in the same attack. Al-Zulfikar claimed responsibility for the attack, and another round of arrests and torture began. The Zia regime seemed unable or unwilling to bring Benazir Bhutto to public trial. Possibly they were worried about antagonizing the United States with another mock trial. For whatever reason, Benazir Bhutto was never tortured to get a confession linking her to Al-Zulfikar, nor was she ever charged with any crimes.

On December 27, 1981, Benazir Bhutto was released from Karachi Central Jail and moved to the Bhutto home of Al-Murtaza at Larkana which again became a subjail. Her isolation at Al-Murtaza was almost as great as it had been in Sukkur Prison. Only her mother and sister were allowed to visit her, and they both lived in Karachi, which is 315 kilometers away from Larkana. Sanam was able to make the trip only twice, and her mother's failing health made it impossible for her to travel.

What was thought to have been tuberculosis while Nusrat Bhutto was in Karachi Central Jail turned out to be a malignant tumor in her right lung. Nusrat Bhutto's doctor in Karachi wanted her to seek medical attention outside the country and assisted her in applying for permission to leave. Permission was denied. The government claimed that Nusrat Bhutto was not ill.

The pressure to allow Nusrat Bhutto to leave Pakistan to seek medical attention for her lung cancer increased both inside Pakistan and in the world community. General Zia was unmoved and continued to tell the world that Nusrat

Bhutto was not ill. In November 1982, the Zia regime convened a medical review board to examine the facts in Nusrat Bhutto's case. The board was supposed to act as a rubber stamp to the government's attempts to keep Nusrat Bhutto in Pakistan. However, her personal physician was appointed to the board and refused to endorse the government's actions. The other doctors went along with him, and the major general in charge of the board finally consented to allow Nusrat Bhutto to leave the country. She left Pakistan on November 20, 1982, while Zia was on a state tour of Southeast Asia. When General Zia returned, the major general who had freed Nusrat Bhutto was stripped of both his military and civilian ranks.

Benazir Bhutto had been allowed to travel to Karachi to say good-bye to her mother and was then allowed to stay at 70 Clifton, which continued to be surrounded by soldiers. The phone lines were routed through a security post and were controlled by the police. They often shut the phones off completely, would only let certain calls get through, or would disconnect Benazir Bhutto in the middle of a conversation.

During this time her chronic ear condition worsened. Benazir Bhutto's doctor treated her as best he could with the limited medical facilities that he could carry into 70 Clifton. He was not permitted to move her to a hospital and, as the condition worsened, Benazir Bhutto began to lose her hearing. The doctor knew that if the ear problems were to be solved, they would require an operation. He recommended to the Zia government that Benazir Bhutto be allowed to travel to London for an operation on her ear. All through 1983, Benazir Bhutto was held at 70 Clifton in need of medical attention. The increasing unrest within Pakistan convinced General Zia that it would be a mistake to allow Benazir Bhutto out of the country where she could speak out against him.

When General Zia traveled to Washington to lobby for more military aid and spoke before the Senate Foreign Relations Committee, Senator Pell inquired about the status and condition of Benazir Bhutto. Apparently General Zia got very angry and told the senator that Benazir Bhutto lived in a house much grander than any house of the senators present. He went on to say that she was permitted visitors, had TV, radio, and a phone. Peter Galbraith was still working for the Foreign Relations Committee and tried to call Benazir Bhutto while the committee met. He was not permitted to talk to her.

Despite well-documented human rights abuses on the part of the Zia government, the Reagan administration continued to give General Zia its wholehearted support. General Zia had become a key player in the worldwide conflict between the United States and the Soviet Union. As long as General Zia remained in power, the United States could continue to aid the Afghan rebels. Many feel that the United States was trying to make Afghanistan the sort of long-drawn-out no-win situation that it had experienced in Vietnam.

Toward the end of 1983, it was finally decided by the government that they would allow Benazir Bhutto to leave the country. She made preparations with mixed emotions. Since General Zia ousted her father in June 1977, she had worked to return democracy to Pakistan. Even when she had been in solitary confinement in Sukkur Prison, she had been a symbol of opposition to the Zia government. Leaving the country, even for the legitimate reason that she was in need of medical attention, seemed in some ways like she was abandoning the cause of the Pakistan People's Party and the Movement to Restore Democracy.

If she didn't have the operation on her infected ear, she was told she could lose her hearing. The infection might spread, causing nerve damage elsewhere. She had already begun experiencing difficulty with her balance. There were a number of false starts: Benazir Bhutto and her sister Sanam would make reservations and then have them canceled by the government. Finally, they were permitted to board an Air France flight at 2:30 A.M. on January 10, 1984. Five-and-a-half years of persecution and incarceration ended, and Benazir Bhutto was finally truly free for the first time since her arrest on September 29, 1979.

In Exile

As Benazir Bhutto left Pakistan, her future was uncertain. But her resolve to continue the fight against General Zia was as strong as ever. Her flight took her to Geneva, Switzerland, where her mother was living in exile. It was a joyous family reunion heightened by a phone call from her brothers Shah Nawaz and Mir Murtaza Bhutto. She had had no direct contact with her brothers since they had left Pakistan shortly after Zulfikar Ali Bhutto had been deposed in 1977. Her brothers had married sisters while they were living in Afghanistan and were now living in France. Mir Murtaza Bhutto visited Benazir Bhutto the next day in Geneva and brought his eighteen-month-old daughter, Fathi, to see her aunt. As much as Benazir Bhutto relished being reunited with her family, it was imperative that she continue on to London for her ear operation.

London was also the most logical place for any concerted efforts against General Zia. There are close to 400,000 Pakistanis in England, many of whom had fled the jails and tortures of the Zia government. At first, Benazir Bhutto was planning to have her ear operated on and then to return to Pakistan as soon as she could. She felt it was her responsibility as the spiritual leader of the movement to oust Zia that she be as close to the action as possible. But events forced her to reconsider.

After the successful ear operation, Benazir's recovery was slow and painful. The doctor who operated on her felt that he might have to do a follow-up operation in nine months to a year. There would be no way for him to do that if Benazir Bhutto returned to Pakistan and, most likely, to imprisonment. Her arrival in England had caused such a stir among the overseas Pakistanis that General Zia would most likely not let her leave again. It also quickly became apparent that she could accomplish much more in the court of world opinion free in London than jailed in Pakistan. In London she would be free to focus world attention on the plight of those still in the jails of General Zia.

When she was strong enough to continue the fight, she moved into an apartment in the Barbican, a well-known apartment building in London. Her apartment became the unofficial foreign headquarters of the Pakistan People's Party. It was from here that Benazir Bhutto waged a war of words against General Zia and his henchmen. She took up the plight of a number of political prisoners who were loyal to her father's memory and the party.

The spare bedroom in Benazir Bhutto's apartment was used as an office. Benazir Bhutto and those who supported her set up a letter-writing campaign and elaborate information-gathering networks so that they could stay abreast of the situation in General Zia's jails. There were few victories during this time. At the same time, there were those within her party who were not above using the situation to try to further their personal goals.

The Pakistan People's Party had always been a diverse coalition of groups and interests held together at first by

On the fifth anniversary of her father's death, Benazir Bhutto addresses a meeting of the Pakistan People's Party in London. The band on her arm reads Long Live Bhuttoism.

the charisma of their leader, Zulfikar Ali Bhutto, and then by their opposition to General Zia. In London, Benazir Bhutto was forced to deal as best she could with the various factions of the party. It was an effrontery to her dedication to the cause that many of the leaders of the party seemed more concerned with their own positions than with the plight of their brethren suffering in the jails of Pakistan. Many of these men had held high positions within her father's government and must have found it difficult to try to negotiate for power with Zulfikar Ali Bhutto's thirty-year-old daughter.

Benazir Bhutto was relentless in her efforts on behalf of those still in Pakistan. She traveled throughout Europe speaking with sympathetic people in and out of government, and with those Pakistanis who lived in Europe. Because of her efforts, Benazir Bhutto received an invitation to speak to the Carnegie Endowment for International Peace in Washington, D.C., in April 1985. She accepted the invitation and used the opportunity, with the assistance of her friend Peter Galbraith, to lobby in Washington against the Zia government and for human rights in Pakistan.

Benazir Bhutto was given the opportunity to speak before the Senate Foreign Relations Committee, where she thanked Senators Pell and Percy for their efforts on her behalf and described for the committee the conditions within Pakistan. At that time the Senate was debating whether to continue aid to Pakistan despite the country's continuing efforts to develop nuclear weapons. Earlier, the Reagan administration had been able to circumvent the law which prohibits the United States from giving military aid to any country that has not signed the Nuclear Non-Proliferation Treaty. Benazir Bhutto said to the committee that cutting off aid would help no one and that aid should be linked to human rights. Pakistan did get its aid, but the United States did nothing to stem the tide of repression that kept Zia in power and his political adversaries in jail or in exile.

In addition to her visit to Washington, she was invited to speak before the European Parliament. She traveled to Strasbourg, France, in June 1985, where she again stated her case against the Zia regime and for a return to democracy in Pakistan. Although the European Parliament has little in the way of real political power, Benazir Bhutto found many sympathetic listeners among its members.

When in London, Benazir Bhutto continued to lead the Pakistan People's Party in the fight against the Zia regime. The bitter lesson that she and her colleagues learned was that Zia was impervious to pressure from the world community. As long as the United States saw him as the front-line defense against the Soviet Union, he could do as he wished. To try and keep the opposition to Zia alive, Benazir Bhutto, along with Bashir Riaz and the others who were helping her in London, published a magazine in Urdu, the official language of Pakistan. Called *Amal* (which means action), the magazine was distributed to organizations and governments who might be able to put pressure on General Zia and/or the media. It was also distributed among the Pakistani community around the world and smuggled into Pakistan. *Amal* even found its way into the hands of the prisoners it was trying to save, and must have given them hope in a nearly hopeless situation.

But it was not easy getting out the magazine. Zia's agents in England would pay the calligraphers (who transcribed the text for the printers) not to work for the magazine. They also tried to influence the printer not to print it.

Despite the attempts by the Zia regime to stop *Amal*, Benazir Bhutto and those working with her were able to keep it going.

Meanwhile, in Pakistan, General Zia was making moves that looked like he intended to return the government to civilian rule. In December 1984 he had held a national vote on a carefully worded referendum. Although many people stayed away from the polls in protest, General Zia called the passage of the referendum a mandate from the people to continue his rule for five more years. General Zia then called for the election of a national assembly, but without a constitution, the national assembly would serve at the whim of General Zia. On February 21, 1985, Benazir Bhutto called for a boycott of the national assembly elections on the grounds that General Zia's ban on the participation of political parties voided the election. The boycott had limited success. However, many of the candidates who were close to General Zia were defeated, including seven members of his cabinet.

In March 1985, General Zia held to his promises and appointed a civilian prime minister, Mohammad Khan Junejo. This was all part of General Zia's plan to appease his critics in the United States Congress. Many members of Congress had become more vocal in their opposition to providing aid to General Zia's military government. Despite the changes, the power of the government still rested firmly in the hands of General Zia, who retained the position of president and army chief of staff.

During this time the activities of Al-Zulfikar tapered off. The Bhutto brothers, Shah Nawaz and Mir Murtaza, had been expelled in 1983 from their base of operations in Afghanistan. They were both still wanted by the Zia government. They had apparently settled down in Europe and were no longer involved with Al-Zulfikar, which had become inactive. Although there has never been any evidence to link Benazir Bhutto or the Pakistan People's Party with Al-Zulfikar, Benazir Bhutto was drawn into the intrigue at a very personal level.

In July 1985 the Bhutto family met for a family vacation on the French Riviera. All four children, Shah Nawaz, Sanam, Mir Murtaza, and Benazir Bhutto were there with their mother. Shah Nawaz, Sanam, and Mir Murtaza all had their spouses and children with them. It was a happy occasion only slightly dampened by the problems that Shah Nawaz was having with his Afghan wife, Rehana. Shah Nawaz had been on the verge of seeking a divorce but had been talked out of it by his eldest sister, Benazir.

After a family cookout on the beach, a night out was planned. All the Bhuttos returned to their different places to change for the evening. Mir Murtaza returned to the small apartment that Benazir Bhutto along with her mother and sister were renting, with the news that Shah Nawaz and Rehana were fighting and would not be joining them. Early the next morning Mir Murtaza returned to his brother's apartment and found him dead. A lengthy investigation followed, and it was determined that Shah Nawaz had been poisoned. On July 18, 1985, the second male member of the Bhutto family died, apparently because of his efforts on behalf of the people of Pakistan.

Shah Nawaz and Mir Murtaza both carried vials of poison so that they could commit suicide if they were ever captured by the Zia regime. The poison, in its undiluted state, would kill almost instantaneously. However, Benazir Bhutto was able to learn from confidential sources that, if diluted, the poison would cause a slow and painful death. The French authorities were able to determine that Shah Nawaz took the poison in a diluted state and that his wife Rehana had been present as he slowly died. She was charged and later convicted in absentia with failing to aid a person in danger. She had fled to the United States. No one was ever charged with administering the poison to him, but his family and many others believe that he was murdered. His family went as far as filing charges of murder (in the French courts) against unknown persons. Many inside and outside of Pakistan believe that the two Afghani sisters who married Shah Nawaz and Mir Murtaza were actually agents of Pakistan's Inter-Services Intelligence.

The death of Shah Nawaz Bhutto set off an emotional outpouring in Pakistan. Thousands of people visited the Bhutto house at 70 Clifton in Karachi to offer prayers to the second martyr of the Bhutto family. In Sind province, where the family burial grounds are located, thousands more people began making their way toward Al-Murtaza in order to attend the upcoming funeral. Government-controlled newspapers that tried to discredit Shah Nawaz Bhutto by claiming he died due to drug and alcohol abuse were burned in protest.

General Zia, whose hold on the country was slipping and who had recently had to squash a coup attempt among his junior officers in the military, stated publicly that Benazir Bhutto was free to return to Pakistan without restrictions. He even went so far as to offer his condolences to the Bhutto family for the death of Shah Nawaz Bhutto. It was hard for anyone in the opposition to trust the word of General Zia, but Benazir Bhutto felt she had to return to Pakistan for her brother's funeral. When she arrived, Gen-

After two years of self-exile, Benazir Bhutto returns to Pakistan to bury her brother Shah Nawaz.

eral Zia had mounted a massive security effort to keep as many people as possible away from Benazir Bhutto and the funeral. He also put many of the Pakistan People's Party leaders in jail so that they would not be able to attend the funeral. General Zia must have felt haunted by the dead Bhuttos as Shah Nawaz's death, as had his father's, became the rallying point for those who opposed the general.

When Benazir Bhutto was finally able to bring Shah Nawaz Bhutto's body back to Pakistan on August 21, 1985, she was greeted at Karachi Airport by one thousand heavily armed soldiers backed up by armored personnel carriers. General Zia had successfully kept the public away from the funeral of Zulfikar Ali Bhutto. This time, however, he was unable to control the masses of people trying to attend.

When Benazir Bhutto landed with the body of her brother at Larkana's Moenjodaro Airport, ten thousand mourners greeted them. The entire eighteen-mile route from the airport to the Bhutto home at Al-Murtaza was lined with people waving black flags of mourning. There were many red, black, and green banners of the outlawed Pakistan People's Party in the crowd as well. The prayer service for men that is part of the Muslim burial ritual had to be held in a sports arena and was attended by twenty-five thousand men. Some observers estimated that as many as fifty thousand people had come to Larkana to attend the funeral.

Following the funeral, Benazir Bhutto pledged her support to the fight to restore democracy in Pakistan. She also declared publicly that she was staying in Pakistan to assume the leadership of the Pakistan People's Party. It seemed that there was an irresistible force driving Benazir Bhutto into the political foreground.

Benazir Bhutto (right) arrives at London's Heathrow Airport hours after being freed from her more-than-two-month house arrest in Karachi. She promised to return to Pakistan as quickly as possible.

After the funeral, Benazir Bhutto, along with a few friends and relatives, returned to 70 Clifton in Karachi. Early on the morning of August 27, 1985, a familiar scene was once again played out. General Zia's police surrounded 70 Clifton, declared it a subjail, and handed Benazir Bhutto a ninety-day detention order. General Zia was unable to keep his promise of no restrictions, and Benazir Bhutto was once again a prisoner of the military government of Pakistan. Benazir Bhutto was held at 70 Clifton until November 3, 1985, when she was permitted to return to France to attend the hearings that would examine the death of her brother. She pledged to the people of Pakistan that she would be back as soon as she could, even if it meant returning to imprisonment.

Home Again

The year 1985 ended on a positive note in Pakistan for those in opposition to General Zia: On December 30, General Zia lifted martial law. Many saw this as another positive step toward a return to democracy. Feeling pressure from the West, General Zia had nine months earlier set up an advisory national assembly. Although political parties were still outlawed, many of the seats in the assembly were won by people loyal to the Pakistan People's Party, and nine of Zia's cabinet members failed to get elected. Many in the opposition refused to participate in Zia's plans as long as he continued to control the military and hold it as a threat over anyone who went too far in questioning the government.

The first real test of Zia's new liberalization came when antigovernment demonstrations broke out throughout the country. The demonstrations on January 5, 1986, marked the fifty-eighth anniversary of the birth of Zulfikar Ali Bhutto. General Zia, still the army chief of staff, kept the troops home and permitted the demonstrators to denounce him and his government. Despite the appearance of the changes, many in the opposition pointed out that General Zia was still firmly in control and could easily reinstate martial law at any time. Benazir Bhutto characterized the changes as cunning camouflage intended to convince the West, especially the United States, that democracy and human rights were returning to Pakistan.

The only way that Benazir Bhutto and her followers in London could test the resolve of the Zia government's move away from martial law and toward democracy was to return to Pakistan and make their demands for total democracy. General Zia had set 1990 as the date for the next national elections. Benazir Bhutto and the Pakistan People's Party, along with the other groups that made up the Movement to Restore Democracy, hoped to force General Zia to schedule elections sooner and to give them the opportunity to defeat him in open and free elections. Shortly after the lifting of martial law, Benazir Bhutto and a number of her followers in London decided they would return to Pakistan. Some of those working with her in London had cases pending against them in Pakistan, and their return would really test Zia's resolve. Benazir Bhutto knew it was a mistake to give General Zia a chance to prepare for her arrival, so the actual date for the trip was kept secret.

Prior to returning to Pakistan, Benazir Bhutto made three trips. She visited Washington, Moscow, and made a religious pilgrimage to Mecca in Saudi Arabia. Benazir Bhutto claims that her trip to Washington was to draw attention to the upcoming test of democracy in Pakistan. Many believe that she also went to Washington to assure those in power that if she were successful in her plan to democratically overthrow General Zia, she would support United States interests in the area. Without at least the tacit approval of Washington, it is doubtful that Benazir Bhutto would have been able to stand up to General Zia.

Her trip to Moscow, at the invitation of a women's organization, was seen as an indication of Benazir Bhutto's political savvy. The visit to Moscow placated many of the left-leaning members of her party who viewed the United States as part of the problem because of their long-term support for General Zia. In addition, it probably strengthened her position with the United States, who would want to keep Benazir Bhutto out of the Soviet sphere of influence.

It was at this time that Benazir Bhutto caught the eye of the media. Her impending—and hopefully triumphant—return to Pakistan made great news. Benazir Bhutto took advantage of the media attention to challenge Zia's guarantees of liberties. She appeared on many television news shows in Europe and the United States and was interviewed by the BBC on the radio. The BBC put her on the air in both English and in Urdu, the official language of Pakistan, for broadcast over the BBC affiliates in Pakistan.

As the preparations for Benazir Bhutto's return proceeded, she began to hear that if she returned to Pakistan, she would be assassinated. Rumors came in from all parts of Pakistan, and one of the Bhutto family servants at 70 Clifton desperately tried to contact Benazir Bhutto in London. When she finally got the message that he had something urgent to tell her and tried to call, she was dismayed to learn that the man and his young niece had been brutally murdered. Considering the number of people that General Zia had had killed because of their opposition to his rule, Benazir Bhutto was wise to take the threats seriously. She couldn't be stopped, though, and on April 11, 1986, she once again returned to Pakistan.

This time there was no veil of mourning. Finally, Benazir Bhutto and the Pakistan People's Party had a position of strength to speak from. They couldn't lose. If General Zia permitted them to speak openly, they would be able to rally the people around their cause and force open and free elections. If General Zia reinstated martial law and tried to smother the opposition, he would prove that his reforms were a farce. Many thought that a return to martial law would send the masses into the street and bring about a violent overthrow of the Zia government. The test was coming, and as Benazir Bhutto and her party members made final arrangements to land in Lahore, the capital of the Punjab and the home of General Zia and many of those in the government and the military, people began to flock to the city.

By the time the Pakistan International Airlines plane landed in Lahore, there were millions of people in the streets of the city. Lahore had taken on the atmosphere of a carnival. After almost nine years of repressive military rule, the people of Pakistan had something to rejoice about. Benazir Bhutto represented the hope for the future. The massive outpouring of emotion and support amazed all: the press, the government, the opposition parties, and Benazir Bhutto were all impressed by the largest gathering in the history of Pakistan. It took the motorcade, carrying Benazir Bhutto on a platform in the back of an open truck, ten hours to travel eight and a half miles from the airport to the site chosen for Benazir Bhutto to speak.

The crowds showered Benazir Bhutto with flower petals and gifts as she traveled to the Minar-i-Pakistan, a monument to Pakistan's independence that had been built while her father was prime minister. In her speech she called for new elections which would be open and free from the type

Opposition leader Benazir Bhutto flashes the victory sign to the crowds that welcomed her home to Pakistan in April 1986.

of restrictions that General Zia had placed on the elections that had selected the current national assembly. She went on to compare General Zia with the recently deposed leader of the Philippines, Ferdinand Marcos. She predicted that Zia would become another Marcos, bowing to the will of the people and leaving the country. Benazir Bhutto had frequently compared herself to Corazon Aquino, who had defeated Marcos after she had taken over her assassinated husband's party. Although the comparison made good copy for the media, it was rather superficial. There were many more differences than similarities between the situation as it had existed in the Philippines and the situation in Pakistan.

Later that week, while Benazir Bhutto was meeting with the leadership of the Pakistan People's Party and other opposition political leaders, armed gunmen broke into the house where Benazir Bhutto was supposed to be. Fortunately, she was elsewhere at the time, but as one member of her party said in describing the gunmen, "They weren't looking for a cup of tea." To capitalize on her overwhelming reception in Lahore, Benazir Bhutto decided to make a tour from Lahore to Peshawar. She wanted to take her message to as many people as possible before the holy month of Ramadan began. During this period of Ramadan, all Muslims are supposed to fast during the day and limit their activities.

During the first few weeks that she was back in Pakistan, Benazir Bhutto began to show a side of herself that surprised many and worried those she opposed. She showed the world that she was able to electrify the huge crowds that greeted her wherever she went, while at the same time she walked a very thin line that held together most of the factions of her party. At the age of thirty-two, Benazir Bhutto was proving herself to be a superior politician. In her speeches she continually called for elections to be scheduled before the planned date of 1990 and presented a balanced and sensible plan for the future of Pakistan. After nine years of being a prisoner and an exile, she amazed the world with her abilities, and many believed that she would be able to ride this wave of support to the leadership of her country.

The old guard of the Pakistan People's Party, many of whom had been supporters of Zulfikar Ali Bhutto, at first saw Benazir Bhutto as a figurehead they could use to rally the masses to the party and against General Zia. However, Benazir Bhutto's success and popularity with the people was so great that she became the actual leader of the party. To solidify her leadership of the party she found it necessary to oust some of the old guard politicians and to replace them with younger members who were loyal to her. This led to some fighting in the party and charges that Benazir Bhutto would turn out to be the same sort of autocratic leader that her father had been and that General Zia was. With her wide appeal among the people, Benazir Bhutto was able to weather the storm within her Party and to solidify its position.

The month of Ramadan lulled the government into a false sense of security, and General Zia's handpicked prime minister, Mohammed Khan Junejo, went so far as to say that Benazir Bhutto and her party had fizzled. It is true that things were quiet during Ramadan, but that was for religious reasons, not because Benazir Bhutto had lost the support of the people. As Ramadan ended, the Pakistan People's Party and the other group involved in the Movement to Restore Democracy renewed their call for elections. They pressed for national elections to be held before the end of 1986.

As Benazir Bhutto and her party began to renew their activities after Ramadan, it became apparent that the fragile, unspoken truce between the Zia government and the opposition was beginning to deteriorate. July 5, 1986, marked the ninth anniversary of General Zia's coup and was declared Black Day by the opposition leaders. Demonstrations were organized all over Pakistan, and in a number of places demonstrators clashed with the police. In Sind, three people were killed and hundreds were wounded when the police fired on the crowds. Elsewhere, others were injured by club-wielding riot police.

The opposition leaders used this as an illustration of the true nature of the Zia regime and proof that General Zia would allow the opposition to protest only under his terms. When both sides planned mass demonstrations for Pakistan Independence Day, August 14, 1986, it appeared that the opposition forces and General Zia were headed for a confrontation.

Benazir Bhutto was reluctant to take her movement into the streets where the peaceful protests she had led would become violent. However, she was maneuvered into leading the Independence Day demonstrations in Karachi by the other leaders of the Movement to Restore Democracy. They put her in the position where if she did not participate it would look like she was bowing to government pressure. At first, Prime Minister Junejo said he would keep his own Pakistan Muslim League members home on Independence Day to avoid a conflict and asked the opposition to do the same. As August 14 approached and it became obvious that the opposition parties were going ahead with their plans, Junejo ordered the demonstrations canceled and placed a three-day ban on public demonstrations. General Zia, in what many viewed as a feeble attempt to make it look as though he wasn't involved in the decisions to limit the rights of the demonstrators, was on a pilgrimage to Mecca at the time. Most believe, however, that Prime Minister Junejo was in frequent contact with General Zia, who was actually running the show from Saudi Arabia.

On August 13, 1986, the inevitable police crackdown on the opposition began. Over one thousand party leaders were arrested and held without being charged with crimes. Out of fear or confusion, Benazir Bhutto was missed in the roundup on August 13, 1986. Some believe that the government did not want to confront Benazir Bhutto and the large contingent of Pakistan People's Party members who surrounded her home at 70 Clifton, which is in an area where there are many foreign embassies and where many foreign diplomats live.

As August 14 dawned, close to five thousand party members had gathered at 70 Clifton in an attempt to protect their leader. Benazir Bhutto awoke on this morning to her followers chanting "Long live Bhutto" and "Our sister Benazir." With the press in a vehicle in front and Benazir in a second vehicle following, the crowd surged into the streets and headed for the market area of Karachi where Benazir Bhutto was scheduled to speak. They had not gone far before the police began their onslaught. The police launched tear gas at the vehicles and unsuccessfully tried to disperse Benazir Bhutto's entourage. In Benazir Bhutto's vehicle they were able to close the windows and sunroof before the gas got to them. Benazir Bhutto was given a wet towel to cover her eyes. However, the sunroof of the vehicle carrying the members of the press jammed, and they received a serious dose of tear gas. Some of the reporters didn't fully recover for a number of months.

By switching vehicles and sending out doubles to elude the police, Benazir Bhutto was able to carry out her Independence Day plans and to speak to the thousands of people who had gathered near the markets to hear her. The police continued their rampage, launching, by some counts, as many as three thousand canisters of tear gas in Karachi alone, where at least four people were killed by police gunfire. There were other incidents of violence throughout the country.

After a day of playing cat and mouse with the police, Benazir Bhutto was arrested late in the afternoon of August 14 during a press conference at 70 Clifton. She was handed a thirty-day detention order and taken off to solitary confinement at Landhi Borstal Jail, which is a juvenile detention center on the outskirts of Karachi. Apparently there was no room for her at Karachi Central Jail, which was overflowing with political prisoners. It was later learned that the orders for her arrest had come by telex directly from General Zia in Saudi Arabia.

Benazir Bhutto's arrest on that day was seen by many as a vindication of her stand that General Zia, along with the police and military, were still running the country and could at any moment return to the repression that had characterized most of Zia's reign. Many in the press saw the harassment and arrest of Benazir Bhutto as a major victory for the opposition. Although the United States government had always been one of Zia's staunchest supporters, in carefully worded statements, United States spokesmen expressed disappointment in the apparent backward step that the Zia government was taking in its process of democratization. They specifically expressed dismay at the arrest and imprisonment of Benazir Bhutto.

In the aftermath of the August 14, 1986, Independence Day demonstrations, the conflict between General Zia and those who opposed him intensified. In the first five days following the arrest and imprisonment of Benazir Bhutto, official sources admitted to twenty-two people having been killed in demonstrations while the opposition claimed as many as forty had been killed by government forces and over ten thousand people arrested. In one incident, train service north of Karachi was disrupted when militants loyal to the opposition sabotaged the train lines.

By August 20, 1986, General Zia once again turned the military against the people of Pakistan. Troops were deployed along the sabotaged rail lines and elsewhere in Sind province. Four top Pakistan People's Party members were charged with murder in the deaths of four people in Lahore. The story had a familiar ring to it. The opposition claimed that the four dead had been part of an antigovernment demonstration and were shot down by police. The police claimed that the opposition leaders shot four progovernment demonstrators.

As the violent demonstrations continued, one thing became clear: Benazir Bhutto's support was strongest in her home province of Sind. The lack of support from the Punjab wing of the party was reopening old wounds caused by earlier ethnic violence and the favoritism that General Zia had shown to his home province of Punjab. It would be Benazir Bhutto's job to heal the wounds within the opposition.

As August 1986 came to an end, General Zia was again firmly in control of Pakistan. Benazir Bhutto and most of her fellow opposition leaders were in jail. Those not in jail were unable or unwilling to risk further deaths, teargassings, and beatings at the hands of the police and the military. At a press conference in Islamabad, Pakistan, on August 30, 1986, General Zia made it clear that he and his supporters in the military had a very limited amount of tolerance for those who wished to speed up the democratization process. He went on to say, without offering any proof, that he had substantiated evidence that Benazir Bhutto was being backed by the Soviet Union. This seemed to many a futile attempt to discredit Benazir Bhutto.

By early September the street violence that had rocked Pakistan for the last two weeks of August had died out. Benazir Bhutto was scheduled to appear in court on September 10 to face charges. On September 9 she was released from jail and allowed to freely return to her home at 70 Clifton. Some claim that General Zia did not want to give her the forum of an open courtroom in which to speak out against him. Many other opposition leaders were released at the same time.

In her first meetings with party members after her release from jail, Benazir Bhutto advocated restraint and hoped that she could lead a movement to bring about change peacefully. Had she done otherwise she could easily have plunged Pakistan into a pattern of escalating violence on both sides. In many ways it would have been easier to

Benazir Bhutto, sitting under a portrait of her father, talks to the media after her release from jail in September 1986.

unleash the masses. It took strong leadership and foresight for Benazir Bhutto to choose the path she did.

The fall was spent solidifying the Pakistan People's Party's internal organization. Benazir Bhutto spent the time touring the country and gathering support for herself and the Pakistan People's Party. In October 1986, Benazir Bhutto announced that she was temporarily canceling her call for immediate elections. Some of the old guard of the Pakistan People's Party split off and formed the National People's Party headed by the former Sind Party leader and general during the reign of Zulfikar Ali Bhutto, Ghulam Mustafa Jatoi.

Ironically, the greatest challenge to the Zia government came not from the political opposition but from ethnically motivated disturbances throughout the country. During the fall, troops had been called upon to deal with ethnic violence in the Northwest Frontier Province, Baluchistan, Lahore, Punjab, and finally in Karachi. The rioting in Karachi apparently began with the attempt by the government to crack down on drug dealers among the Pathan minority. The crackdown set off violence between the Pakhtuns and the Muhajir, people who had moved from India to Pakistan when Pakistan became a country. Before the military was able to establish an uneasy peace in the area, more than 170 people had been killed and 2,000 arrested. The months of ethnic violence culminated in the resignation of all thirty-three members of the federal cabinet and placed the process of returning Pakistan to civilian rule in a doubtful light.

Despite the violence among the various ethnic factions in the country, Benazir Bhutto had much to celebrate as the new year, 1987, dawned. This would be the first New

Benazir Bhutto met with a group of Muslim women supporters and vowed to continue her peaceful opposition to Pakistan's military government.

Year's Eve in six years that she was both free and in Pakistan. Support for her party was growing, and the regime was proving itself unable to run the country without the strong hand of the military. There was, however, one dark cloud on the horizon of the new year. Reports of plans to assassinate Benazir Bhutto became more and more frequent and came from sources inside and outside the government.

During the month of January, the rumors of attacks on Benazir Bhutto and those close to her turned to reality. One of her security guards had his car forced into a dead-end street in Karachi where he was shot at. A Movement to Restore Democracy leader was murdered with an axe. Others among those close to Benazir Bhutto began receiving phone calls in the middle of the night. A direct attack came on January 30, 1987, when Benazir Bhutto's motorcade was attacked by gunmen on the road from Karachi to Larkana at three-thirty in the afternoon. Fortunately, Benazir Bhutto had sent the vehicles on ahead so that she could attend a last-minute meeting in Karachi. The Pajero, a jeeplike vehicle in which Benazir Bhutto always rode, escaped through a shower of bullets. The second vehicle carrying Benazir Bhutto's security staff was stopped, and the people in the car were kidnapped.

The assassination attempt set off another rash of demonstrations against the government. The Zia regime claimed that the attack had been perpetrated by dacoits, highway bandits, common in Pakistan. As there was no ransom demand made, very few found the government's version of the story believable. Those captured in the attack were later released and claimed that their captors said they were working for General Zia.

In many ways, Pakistan was at its lowest point in many years in the early months of 1987. General Zia's plan to return the country to democracy had all but ended. The local elections in the fall of 1986 had been the most corrupt in the history of Pakistan. The hope that General Zia would ever allow free and open elections in 1990 or at any other time seemed dim. Benazir Bhutto, the Pakistan People's Party, and the other groups involved in the Movement to Restore Democracy continued their organizing and resistance to General Zia. The most important thing to happen to Benazir Bhutto in 1987 was in her personal life.

The Marriage of Benazir Bhutto

Benazir Bhutto had always planned to marry. Having experienced the early years of the women's movement at Harvard, she saw no reason why she couldn't have a political career and be a wife and mother. But events interrupted any possibility of her finding the right husband and getting married. During the time her father was on trial and appealing for his life, there were no thoughts of husband hunting. During this time her family did receive inquiries from families with sons who were interested in Benazir Bhutto. Following the death of her father, Benazir Bhutto was in jail and would not have been able to get married had she received any serious proposals. Once she was in exile, however, the inquiries from prominent families began again.

In Pakistan, as in other Muslim countries, there is little opportunity for dating in the Western sense, and arranged marriages are an accepted way for couples to get married. Her father had had an arranged marriage when he had been in his teens and then had later married Benazir Bhutto's mother for love. Her brothers and sister had all married for love. Benazir Bhutto had always expected to follow the rest of her family and to marry for love. Benazir Bhutto's life, however, had not allowed her the luxury of finding someone whom she loved and wanted to marry. Her position as the leader of the Pakistan People's Party made it impossible for her to have any social life. Even the slightest breach of Muslim custom would have been ammunition for General Zia and the government-controlled press.

A possible solution to this dilemma appeared early in the summer of 1985 when Hakim Ali Zardari approached Benazir Bhutto's Aunt Manna, the eldest member of the Bhutto family. He suggested that a marriage be arranged between Benazir Bhutto and his son Asif Zardari. Benazir Bhutto is the same age as Asif Zardari. He had also attended school in England and was from another one of the powerful landowning families of Sind Province. His father had been a supporter of Zulfikar Ali Bhutto and was the vice-president of the Awami National Party, which is one of the parties in the Movement to Restore Democracy.

At the time of the proposal, Asif Zardari ran his family's construction company and played on his own polo team, the Zardari Four. Following the customs of the arranged marriage, Benazir Bhutto's mother and aunt investigated the possibilities of the match. They delved into the Zardari family's history and financial holdings and explored all the aspects of Asif's personality and upbringing. They had even received assurances from the prospective groom that he would not interfere with Benazir Bhutto's political ambitions. Their final conclusion was that Asif Zardari would make the best match possible for Benazir Bhutto.

They approached Benazir Bhutto with the proposal and the recommendation that she accept while they were all in Cannes on the French Riviera in July 1985. The death of her brother Shah Nawaz Bhutto at that time put any thoughts of marriage out of everybody's mind. But Benazir Bhutto's aunt and mother kept the idea of a marriage between Benazir and Asif alive. In November 1986, Benazir Bhutto's Aunt Manna included Asif Zardari on the guest list of a dinner party at 70 Clifton. Without making the connection between the man whose family was trying to arrange a marriage with her and the man that her aunt introduced her to at 70 Clifton, Benazir Bhutto proceeded to get into an argument with him.

As time passed, the Zardaris continued to press for the marriage, as did Benazir Bhutto's mother, sister, and aunts. Finally starting to give in to the pressure applied by her family, Benazir Bhutto began to make inquiries of her own about Asif Zardari. The more she learned about this persistent man, the more the possibility of their getting married became a reality for her. Finally, Benazir Bhutto agreed to meet with her suitor. Unlike most arranged marriages, in this one the prospective bride would have the final say.

The meeting was planned for July 22, 1987, at the apartment of Benazir Bhutto's Aunt Behjat in London. Over the next few days, Asif Zardari and Benazir Bhutto were together, although never alone, at a number of family social gatherings. Finally, Benazir Bhutto, the leader of the opposition to General Zia in Pakistan, educated at Harvard and Oxford, agreed to an arranged marriage with Asif Zardari. Their engagement was announced in London on July 29, 1987. They expected that the wedding would be held before the end of the year.

The road to marriage had been different for Asif Zardari. He had known for many years that he would like to marry Benazir Bhutto. During an interview in London, Asif Zardari surprised Benazir Bhutto by admitting that, when they were both in their early teens, he used to watch her when she came to a movie house that his father owned. He had admired her from afar since that time. Apparently he had told his father five years earlier that if his father wanted him to get married then they should arrange it so he could marry Benazir Bhutto.

The engagement of Asif Zardari and Benazir Bhutto had immediate ramifications for the Zardaris. The Central Bank, which was controlled by the Zia government, canceled loans to the family businesses. The Zia-controlled press printed false stories that were intended to discredit the engaged couple. Rumors were spread that Benazir Bhutto would abandon politics now that she was to be a wife. It was much more wishful thinking on the part of the Zia government than reality. In many ways, being married strengthened Benazir Bhutto's bid to lead her country. She proved to many of her critics that she was more than willing to accept the traditional customs of her country while still trying to bring progress.

After the announcement of their engagement, Benazir Bhutto continued to work as the leader of the Pakistan People's Party. Her goal was to have as large a base of support as possible by the time of the 1990 elections. As Benazir Bhutto traveled about the country, Asif Zardari kept in touch with her by calling frequently. Through the phone calls, they began to get to know each other. They set the date of their wedding for December 19, 1987 and chose to hold it at 70 Clifton, the Bhuttos' home in Karachi.

As the plans became finalized for the wedding, it became apparent that, despite the traditional nature of the arranged wedding, Benazir Bhutto was going to put her own stamp on the proceedings. In Pakistan, families frequently spend their life savings and then go into debt to make a wedding as elaborate as possible. As the leader of a political party that was hoping to improve the lot of people in Pakistan, Benazir Bhutto wanted her wedding to set an example of moderation. She hoped that other people would see that if Benazir Bhutto could cut back on wedding expenses, so could they.

Benazir Bhutto allowed her prospective husband to buy her only two outfits for her trousseau, as opposed to the traditional twenty-one. Rather than wearing solid gold bangles from wrist to elbow as is the custom, Benazir Bhutto wore a few gold bangles and then covered her arms with inexpensive glass bangles that she bought in the bazaars of Karachi. It was also traditional that the bride's wedding outfit be covered with as much gold brocade as possible. Benazir Bhutto told Asif that she wanted her wedding clothes to have brocade only at the top or the bottom but not both. She also asked her prospective husband to show restraint in buying jewelry for her to wear at the wedding. She wanted just a few pieces rather than the lavish amounts that most Pakistani brides wear. She also intended to keep her last name. She felt it necessary as the leader of the party founded by Zulfikar Ali Bhutto to keep the Bhutto name.

The prewedding emotions among the political observers and activists in Pakistan were mixed and often reflected which side of the political battle lines a person was on. Those who supported General Zia and Prime Minister Junejo saw the wedding as Benazir Bhutto's abandonment of her cause. They hoped that as Mrs. Zardari, Benazir Bhutto would fade from the political scene. Most of those who supported her seemed to share in her joy as they would if their sister were getting married. This is how many in the movement saw Benazir Bhutto—a sister who had borne the brunt of the tragedies that had befallen their country since General Zia had taken over. To many it was the unofficial end to the period of mourning that had begun with the execution of Zulfikar Ali Bhutto in 1979. The emotional outpouring surrounding the wedding forces one to conclude that Benazir Bhutto had made the right choice as far as her political life was concerned. The wedding also made Benazir Bhutto more acceptable to many of the more conservative elements in Pakistan who could never have supported her as a single woman in a male-dominated society.

The plans for the wedding included two separate activities. The first was a private wedding for two thousand people to be held in a tented garden near 70 Clifton. The second was a public reception in the sports stadium in Lyari, a poverty-stricken area of Karachi that is a Pakistan People's Party stronghold and the site of Benazir Bhutto's Independence Day speech on August 14, 1986. Because of her sisterly image, most of the young men who made up the bulk of the Party felt they should be invited to their "sister's" wedding. The reception at Lyari was intended to include as many supporters as possible. For the first time since 1977, the Pakistan People's Party would have something to celebrate.

The private part of the wedding, despite Benazir Bhutto's attempts to tone it down, was a lavish affair attended by many of the wealthiest people in Pakistan. The guest list also included three of Benazir Bhutto's friends from the United States and six from her days at Oxford. As if to highlight the public nature of Benazir Bhutto's life, she held a press conference the morning of the wedding. She wanted to explain to the reporters that had flocked to Pakistan what her plans were and why she had decided to go ahead with her marriage. Benazir Bhutto stressed that she did not expect those from the West to understand her motivations for accepting an arranged marriage. She explained that her choice was not between an arranged marriage or a Western-style romantic marriage but between an arranged marriage or no marriage at all. She further explained that she had an obligation to her family and the customs of her country to marry and have a family.

On the subject of a family, she said that Asif wanted a large family, but that they would wait to have children until after the 1990 elections. She did relate to the reporters that one of her friends had told her that the best way for Benazir Bhutto to get General Zia to call for early elections was to become pregnant as soon after the wedding as possible.

The wedding consisted of two days of ceremonies that are traditional to Muslim weddings. After the actual vows were said on the second day and the invited guests were greeted at the reception by the newlyweds, Benazir Bhutto and her new husband headed for Lyari. At the public reception, over one hundred thousand people had assembled to celebrate the marriage of Asif Zardari and Benazir Bhutto. One reporter stated that it was more like a rock concert than a wedding reception. The newly married couple sat on a stage that had been specially built for the occasion. They were dressed in the matching white tunics that they had been married in. The massive crowd shared the joy of the day and celebrated as fireworks burst in the sky above. Many of the celebrants waved their rifles in the air as they danced and fired their rifles into the skies.

One person attending the reception was killed by a stray bullet, and thirty people were injured in the crush to get close to the newlyweds. If the reception at Lyari was any indication of how the rank and file was going to react to the wedding of their leader, then it was clear that the people were happy with Benazir Bhutto's choice in her arranged marriage to Asif Zardari.

1988—The Year of Victory

The first few months of 1988 saw Pakistan become increasingly unstable. Violence was becoming a way of life for much of the country as various factions clashed. More than one hundred people died in the Northwest Frontier Province area of Gilgit when Sunni and Shiite Muslim groups fought. As many as 100 people were killed in one day of fighting between native Pakhtun tribesmen and Muhajirs, descendants of the Indian Muslims who chose to settle in Pakistan when it was created in 1947. In various locations, the military had been confronted by civilians who were disgruntled with the military's role in police activities.

The enthusiasm over Benazir Bhutto and Asif Zardari's marriage was again proof of the people's support of Benazir.

In some parts of the country, drug dealers and smugglers with automatic weapons were in control. The expanding drug trade during the almost eleven years of General Zia's reign had increased the number of heroin addicts from a few thousand in 1977 to nearly a million in 1988. Through all of this, recently married Benazir Bhutto continued to organize and strengthen her Pakistan People's Party. The party had suffered a serious blow in the November 1987 local elections, when they only had a strong showing in rural Sind districts. It was Benazir Bhutto's intention to get the Pakistan People's Party in a position to beat Prime Minister Junejo and President (General) Zia in the next scheduled elections in 1990.

Many people in and out of Pakistan doubted that General Zia would ever permit open and free elections. They felt this was especially true if it meant that Benazir Bhutto would end up in a position where she would have a say in the running of the country. During this time, Benazir Bhutto and her followers challenged General Zia in every way they could. The general tried to force all political parties to register and to be approved by his government. Benazir Bhutto took her case to the Pakistani Supreme Court and challenged his right to do that under the current constitution. In a ruling in February 1988, which set the court in opposition to the man who had appointed them, the Pakistani Supreme Court ruled in favor of Benazir Bhutto and the Pakistan People's Party.

General Zia was slowly losing control of the country that he had single-handedly run for almost eleven years. His handpicked prime minister and national assembly that existed at his discretion were pushing for a greater role in governing the country. On May 29, 1988, in what appeared to many to be a last-ditch effort to hang on to his power, General Zia brought the country back under his sole domination. Prime Minister Junejo returned from an overseas trip to be greeted by the announcement that General Zia was relieving him of his duties. He also dismissed the entire cabinet and dissolved the National Assembly. General Zia cited the inability of the Junejo government to handle the increasing violence in the country as the reason for their dismissal. He also claimed that there was widespread corruption in the government. The violence was self-evident, and the corruption was highly probable. In published reports, it had been repeatedly claimed that about two-thirds of the aid for the Afghan rebels were being siphoned off in Pakistan before it reached those it was intended to help. It seemed that the main reason for the shake-up was that General Zia and his military backers were unable to share control of the country with civilian authority.

There was another catalyst for the dissolution of the government and the promise of elections as outlined in the constitution. Four days earlier, a Karachi paper had leaked the news that Benazir Bhutto was pregnant and that the baby was due in the fall. If the elections came at about the same time the baby was due, Benazir Bhutto's ability to campaign would be greatly diminished. Without her visibly at the head of the campaign, the Pakistan People's Party's effect on national elections would be greatly diminished. The world will never know for sure if General Zia was motivated to act by the announcement that Benazir Bhutto was pregnant, but it seems a strange coincidence.

In mid-June, in another move that might be interpreted as an attempt to block the campaign of Benazir Bhutto,

General Zia declared a change in the basic laws of Pakistan. He put Pakistani law under the auspices of the religious leaders. Had this move been successful, General Zia would have turned Pakistan into another religious state like the Islamic Republic of Iran. Under the Shariah, Islamic law, the role of women in Pakistan would have been greatly diminished. The Shariah states that women are not permitted to work outside the home and must be fully covered when they leave their homes. General Zia had been pushing the country toward becoming a fundamentalist Islamic state during his entire reign. Yet this was such a drastic move and so poorly planned that even few of his supporters among the religious conservatives were able to support his call for Shariah. Loudest among the opposition to General Zia's call for Shariah were the various women's organizations in Pakistan who had fought hard for their rights in a male-dominated society. It seemed that General Zia had lost much of the political expertise that had kept him in power for eleven years. Reporters found him lacking confidence and indecisive in his press conferences.

Benazir Bhutto and those in the opposition began to prepare for the elections. They called for outside observers to insure that General Zia kept his promise of open and free elections. Benazir Bhutto's pregnancy also continued, with the due date a carefully guarded secret. Benazir Bhutto carried her medical records with her so that the secret police would not be able to get them from her doctor's office. The truth was that the baby was due in mid-October, but Zia's intelligence forces estimated that the due date was November 17. General Zia scheduled elections for November 16, 1988.

By the beginning of August 1988, it looked as though

the Pakistan People's Party candidates would be winners in any fairly held election. Many candidates who had been in the National Assembly that General Zia dissolved, switched from former Prime Minister Junejo's Muslim League to the Pakistan People's Party. They did this so that their names on the ballot would be accompanied by the symbol for the Pakistan People's Party. In a country where as many as 80 percent of the population is illiterate, the symbols on the ballot are extremely important. General Zia wanted to try to prevent a sweep by the Pakistan People's Party and to be forced to share the government with Benazir Bhutto. He declared as he had done in 1985 that the fall elections would be conducted on a nonparty basis. This turned out to be another miscalculation on the part of General Zia, as it unified the opposition against him. With Benazir Bhutto in the vanguard, the opposition called on the Supreme Court to rule on General Zia's attempt once again to ban political parties.

Many in Pakistan thought the pattern of Pakistan history was repeating itself and that either General Zia or someone else in the military would return the country to martial law rather than let a liberal civilian government come to power. The conditions in the country were such that the continuation of aid from the United States was in jeopardy. Many in the government and especially the military had legally and illegally gotten rich from the billions of dollars that had been poured into Pakistan by the United States to support General Zia in his position against the expansion of communism in Southwest Asia. As the situation neared the boiling point in August 1988, one as yet unexplained event radically changed the power struggle within Pakistan.

On August 17, 1988, General Zia, accompanied by the United States Ambassador to Pakistan, Arnold Raphel, U.S. Brigadier General Herbert Wassom, the United States military attaché in Pakistan, and a number of high-ranking Pakistani military officials, were killed in a plane crash. The group had attended a demonstration of the United States–made Abrams M–1 tanks in Bahawalpur, 330 miles south of Islamabad and were returning to the capital. Shortly after takeoff, at 3:46 P.M., observers on the ground claimed to have seen black smoke coming from the plane's fuselage. Then the plane literally fell out of the sky. When it hit the ground, it bounced twice and then on the third bounce burst into flames. The fire was so hot that no one could get near the plane. All thirty people on board perished in the crash.

Theories on what happened abound. General Zia had many enemies, and most believe that some sort of foul play was involved. Many theories have come out as to who was responsible for the crash and why. The Soviet Union was suspected because of their anger regarding General Zia and the United States aiding the mujahedin in Afghanistan. The Soviet-backed regime in Kabul, Afghanistan, was suspected for the same reason. Some suggested that factions within India could have benefited from the death of General Zia and the chaos it might cause in Pakistan. Many Indians believed that General Zia was arming Sikh rebels in Pakistan and helping them in their campaign against the Indian government. There were also many suspects within Pakistan. Members of the military had staged at least one unsuccessful coup attempt against General Zia in the early 1980s. This possibility was given weight by the fact that factions within the military would have found it easiest to sabotage the plane. Mir Murtaza Bhutto, Benazir Bhutto's brother, may have been responsible. Mir Murtaza Bhutto had stated that he had tried five times to have General Zia killed. Maybe his sixth attempt was successful. The list goes on to include a number of ethnic and political factions in Pakistan and even the U.S. Central Intelligence Agency. A thorough investigation has never been completed, and it is unlikely that we will ever know the whos, whys, or hows surrounding the death of General Zia. We can, however, assess the results of his death and the impact it had on Pakistani politics.

Under the Pakistan constitution, the president of the Senate is next in line to the presidency. Ghulam Ishaq Khan was the man who was president of the Senate when General Zia had dismissed the government in May. He became the acting president until a new government could be formed following the November elections. As many of the top military commanders had been on the plane with General Zia, there was confusion in the military as well. Acting President Ishaq Khan appointed General Mirza Aslam Beg to the post of army chief of staff, the position that General Zia had been given by Zulfikar Ali Bhutto. An advisory council was set up consisting of Acting President Ishaq Khan, General Beg, and other current and former officials. This may have been the most critical time in the history of Pakistan. It amazed many observers that Pakistan stayed calm following the death of General Zia. Two hundred thousand attended General Zia's funeral on August 21, 1988, in Islamabad. Among them was Secretary of State George P. Shultz, who represented the United States.

Many observers inside and outside Pakistan expected the

military to take over and to continue to run the country, as it had done a number of times in the past. Others saw this as the first real opportunity for democracy in Pakistan. The death of General Zia also created a dilemma for Benazir Bhutto.

She and the Pakistan People's Party had been fueled for the last eleven years by one primary goal: the removal of General Zia from power and the restoration of democracy. The plane crash eliminated the major issue of the party and forced the elections into a debate based much more on issues. At the same time Benazir Bhutto was forced to direct some attention to her pregnancy. Shortly after the death of General Zia, she became worried about the well-being of her unborn baby.

She felt that the baby was not moving around enough in the womb. Apparently, the seemingly endless meetings were taking their toll. Toward the end of August, after one meeting that lasted exceptionally long, Benazir Bhutto felt ill and went to the doctor for a checkup. Rather than visit one of the doctors who catered to the wealthy people of the Clifton area of Karachi, Benazir Bhutto had selected a doctor at Lady Dufferin Hospital in the Lyari section of Karachi. The poor people of Lyari had been the stalwarts of the Pakistan People's Party. Benazir Bhutto wanted to show them that the hospital in their part of town was as good as any.

When Benazir Bhutto went to the doctor, he did an ultrasound, which showed that there was too little amniotic fluid in the womb. This condition was preventing the baby from moving as much as it should. The doctor suggested that all the time spent sitting in meetings was causing Benazir Bhutto to have poor circulation. He had

Benazir Bhutto spend the next four days in bed. She was then to follow a regimen of spending one hour each morning resting and trying to feel the baby move. She was told that if she couldn't feel the baby move, then she was to go immediately to the hospital. The doctor also wanted her to come to his office every four days so they could do a fetal stress test.

On September 19, 1988, during a regular checkup, the doctor said that Benazir Bhutto had another three or four weeks to go before the baby was due. The following day, when a fetal stress test was done, the doctor admitted her to the hospital. A seven-pound baby boy was born on the morning of September 21, 1988, by cesarean section. The happy parents named their new son Bilawal, which means "one without equal." As soon as she was able after the birth of her son, Bilawal Ali Zardari, Benazir Bhutto was back on the campaign trail.

On October 2, 1988, the Supreme Court of Pakistan ruled that political parties would be allowed to participate in the upcoming elections. The caretaker government of Ishaq Khan accepted the ruling. It seemed that even the natural environment was testing the people of Pakistan as floods swept down the Indus Valley and engulfed Lahore. In one area the government dynamited a flood-control dike flooding one of the poorer sections of the city in an attempt to save a wealthy part of the city. The people of the country were outraged.

The violence that had been plaguing the country flared again in October 1988. In early November Benazir Bhutto's mother, Nusrat Bhutto, was shot at while campaigning in Multan. This and other incidents caused many of those on the campaign trail to fear that the military would step

Benazir Bhutto reads to her son,
Bilawal Ali Zardari.

in. However, under the leadership of General Beg, the army stayed away from the political arena. They seemed to be willing to let the election process run its course. With more than thirty registered political parties, the campaign became hectic as parties and candidates switched alliances and sides, trying to improve their chances in the elections. The coalition of parties that made up the Movement to Restore Democracy had a falling-out. The Pakistan People's Party was suddenly thrust from opposition status to front-runner. Now they were the party to beat, and many of the other parties were negotiating an alliance against them. Many were speculating that Benazir Bhutto would be the next prime minister, even though she had had to leave the campaign trail to have her baby and to overcome a kidney infection that followed.

As the elections drew closer, it became clear that it was going to be primarily a two-party race between Benazir Bhutto and the Pakistan People's Party and former Prime Minister Mohammed Khan Junejo, Milan Nawaz Sherif, and a coalition of right-leaning parties called the Islamic Democratic Alliance. The Muslim League was at the head of the alliance. The positions of the two main parties were really not that different. Both called for a better life for the poor, continued support of the Afghan rebels, close ties to the United States, nuclear power for peaceful means only, and civilian rule unhindered by the military. One area they differed over was the extent to which the country should be run according to Islamic law. The Muslim League and its Islamic Democratic Alliance were for the continued Islamization of the country. Benazir Bhutto felt that there should be a separation of church and state. She was especially fearful that women would suffer under strict adherence to Islamic law. The main issue of the election in many ways became one of loyalty to two dead former leaders of Pakistan. Those loyal to the memory of Zulfikar Ali Bhutto would vote for the Pakistan People's Party candidates led by Benazir Bhutto. Those loyal to the memory of General Zia would vote for the Muslim League and its Islamic Democratic Alliance led by former Prime Minister Junejo. Despite everything, there were many in Pakistan who had prospered under the rule of General Zia and felt that his type of autocratic rule was needed in order for the country to remain stable. As the campaign went on, many candidates who had been loyal to General Zia tried to disassociate themselves from him.

Not having held open and free elections for over eleven years, there were no facilities or expertise in the area of pre-election polling. As the elections approached, it was hard for the media to read the electorate accurately. Many people suggested that at best the Pakistan People's Party would have a clear majority in the 237-seat National Assembly. Others expected that they might not have a majority of the seats but that they would win more seats than any of the other parties. The election process was further complicated by a separate vote for the provincial assemblies where a total of 483 seats were up for grabs. The national elections would be held on Wednesday, November 16, 1988, with the provincial elections to be held on Saturday, November 19, 1988.

As the results were tallied from the voting on November 16, it became clear that Benazir Bhutto's eleven-year quest to return Pakistan to democracy was finally succeeding. The Pakistan People's Party won 92 of the 217 seats that were to be chosen in the election for the National Assem-

November 1988: Casting a vote for the first time in her life, Benazir Bhutto votes in the first free election held in Pakistan in over eleven years.

bly. The Islamic Democratic Alliance, the second largest winner, only got 55. The remaining 70 seats were scattered among a vast array of parties with the recently formed Mohajir Quami Movement coming in a surprising but distant third with thirteen seats. An additional twenty seats in the National Assembly are reserved specifically for women and were to be chosen later.

Without a clear majority for the Pakistan People's Party, it fell to Acting President Ishaq Khan to decide whom he would ask to form the new government. As Ishaq Khan delayed his decision, the Islamic Democratic Alliance and the Pakistan People's Party headed by Benazir Bhutto vied for the support of the seventy noncommitted members of the National Assembly. After the women's seats were apportioned, the Pakistan People's Party controlled 105 of the 237 seats in the National Assembly and had the support of enough independent candidates to be able to command a majority. On December 1, 1988, President Ishaq Khan invited Benazir Bhutto to become prime minister and to form a new government. In his public address to the country, President Ishaq Khan said that Benazir Bhutto had "the best qualities of leadership and foresight as a statesman." He went on to say that, "Ms. Benazir Bhutto has the country's love in her heart." His announcement officially ended the rule of the deceased General Zia and his military allies. Although Zulfikar Ali Bhutto had been the first elected prime minister of Pakistan, he had originally come to power at the invitation of the military. Benazir Bhutto became the first head of Pakistan to assume power through the electoral process.

Madame Prime Minister

On December 2, 1988, Benazir Bhutto was sworn in as the prime minister of Pakistan, setting many firsts. She was the first woman to lead a modern Muslim nation. She was the first person to lead Pakistan through totally open and free elections. And she became the youngest current head of state in the world. Many people throughout the country were jubilant as she assumed her position as the duly elected leader of Pakistan. Ironically, this was the first paying job Benazir Bhutto had ever held.

The people of Pakistan truly had reason to celebrate. The swearing-in of Benazir Bhutto heralded a new era for Pakistan. But there was also reason for concern: Benazir Bhutto and the Pakistan People's Party would have to depend on a coalition of independent and lesser party assembly members to keep the government together. Most threatening of all were the conditions within the country. Benazir Bhutto was faced with a number of problems, all demanding attention. On the eve of her taking office, Pakistan was on the brink of bankruptcy. The International Monetary Fund was demanding certain concessions from

The swearing-in of Prime Minister Benazir Bhutto was the culmination of years of work and sacrifice by many people.

Pakistan in exchange for the loans needed to get the country out of its current crisis. To placate the military, Benazir Bhutto had assured them that she would not tamper with military spending which was chewing up between 40 and 60 percent of Pakistan's budget. She had promised her supporters that she would work for improvements in the area of social reform and services. Unfortunately, she was faced with a budget in which the percentage of expenditure for social services was among the lowest in the world. Health care, housing, land reform, education, civil rights, and freedom of the press were all areas that cried out from eleven years of neglect by the military dictatorship of General Zia.

It was also up to Benazir Bhutto to deal with the drug problems within Pakistan and the bands of drug smugglers that had expanded during the Zia years. Speaking several days after her swearing-in, Prime Minister Bhutto stated that drugs were the number one problem in Pakistan. She also had to keep a lid on the ethnic violence that had always plagued the country and had been exceptionally bad in the last years that General Zia was in power. As part of the ethnic problem, she also had to somehow solve the problems created by three million Afghan refugees living in Pakistan, mostly along the Afghan-Pakistan border.

Internationally, Benazir Bhutto was also walking a thin line. The United States expected her support in its ongoing policy of aiding the Afghan rebels. The United States also wanted assurances that she would not pursue the Pakistani nuclear weapon program that had been started by her father and continued in secret by General Zia. The long-standing tensions between India and Pakistan were a perennial problem. The two countries had gone to war with each other three times since 1947.

To keep all the factions and problems within and outside Pakistan from tearing down the fragile democratic government, Benazir Bhutto had to prove that she could be as successful leading a country as she had been in leading the opposition. Her charismatic appeal to the people would have to be accompanied by a pragmatic ability to manage a country of 107 million people on a day-to-day basis. Many thought the task was beyond the ability of anyone. One member of the opposition, Ms. Abida Hussein, said on the television news show *60 Minutes* that "if Benazir Bhutto had a perfect head, perfect heart, and a perfect soul she'd probably still fail."

In her first speech as prime minister, Benazir Bhutto said, "We will choose the path of love. We will eradicate hunger and poverty. We will provide shelter for the homeless. We will provide employment for the unemployed. We will educate the illiterates." She went on to promise that women will be given full partnership in Pakistan. One of her first official acts was the freeing of one thousand prisoners still in General Zia's jails. Most of those freed were political prisoners. She then lifted curbs on student and labor unions that had been instituted during the days of martial law. One journalist likened the mood in Pakistan to the "Camelot" atmosphere of the Kennedy White House in the early 1960s.

The people of Pakistan basked in the newfound openness of the government of Benazir Bhutto. For the first time in eleven years they could openly talk politics. Even the opposition leaders were granted time on government-run television to criticize Benazir Bhutto and her government. This was a right that not even her father had granted his opposition. One Western journalist who had lived in Pakistan and had been expelled by the government in 1982, returned in December 1988. He found Pakistan a radically different place. People were open and willing to talk. The fear that had gripped the country under martial law had vanished.

The next order of business for the government was electing a president. Under the Pakistan constitution, the presidency is primarily a ceremonial position with the real power of the government resting with the prime minister. Acting President Ishaq Khan was the only serious candidate. He received the backing of both the Pakistan People's Party and the Islamic Democratic Alliance. When the election was held, he won 78 percent of the vote.

The Pakistani constitution also required that a new government undergo a vote of confidence in the National Assembly within the first sixty days after taking office. On December 12, 1988, Prime Minister Bhutto put herself and her party up to the vote. They received 148 votes in favor of their government and only 55 no-confidence votes.

Benazir Bhutto was quickly thrust into the international spotlight as well. Her long struggle against General Zia, her imprisonments and exile gave her victory a fairy-tale quality that captured the imagination of the world press. She appeared on the cover of magazines throughout the world.

The scheduled three-day summit of the South Asian Association for Regional Cooperation (SAARC) December 29–31, 1988, would be Benazir Bhutto's first opportunity to interact with her fellow leaders of the neighboring South Asian states. Foremost among these would be Rajiv Gandhi, the prime minister of India. He would be the first Indian prime minister to visit Pakistan since his grandfather, Jawaharlal Nehru, visited in 1960. Gandhi's cooperation in reducing tensions between Pakistan and India would be very helpful to both leaders.

The results of the SAARC conference were considered a success for Benazir Bhutto. India and Pakistan signed a bilateral agreement stating that neither would attack the other's nuclear power installations. The conference as a whole reached agreement on cooperation and the sharing of intelligence in the ongoing fight against the drug trade in the area. The participants also reached a consensus on a number of issues that had to be dealt with during the next decade. The plan, called SAARC 2000, addresses many of the social ills that the 1.1 billion people of South Asia face.

The first few months of 1989 were marked by a lack of action on the part of the Bhutto government. Benazir Bhutto and the Pakistan People's Party had failed to present a single piece of legislation. Benazir Bhutto had done everything she could that did not cost money: freeing prisoners, lifting the ban on unions, permitting freedom of the press. Yet she was unable to come up with funding for any new programs. Her hands were tied by the concessions that had been made to the International Monetary Fund to get $800 million in loans. Despite the lack of action, her popularity among the people remained solid. Benazir Bhutto was maintaining the delicate balance within the country, trying to placate as many groups as possible. It seemed that the easiest way to do that was to do very little.

Prime Minister Bhutto's attempts at maintaining a balance among the factions in Pakistan met with mixed re-

Prime Minister Bhutto chaired the concluding session of the seven-nation SAARC conference.

sults. As in all political situations, each faction had its own ideas about how things should be done. The two most serious opposition factions were the religious fundamentalists and the provincial government of the Punjab led by Nawaz Sherif and the Islamic Democratic Alliance. Both tested the ability of the prime minister to weather political storms.

The most conservative among the religious leaders went so far as to claim that a woman, under Islamic law, was ineligible to lead a country. They called for the immediate removal of Prime Minister Bhutto. The Prime Minister met the challenge head on declaring that Islam is a religion, not a government. She also went on to state that she would do everything in her power to see that the women of Pakistan got equal rights under the law.

The challenge from Nawaz Sherif, who was seen by many as in league with the conservative religious leaders, was in many ways more serious. As the head of the provincial government of the Punjab, Nawaz Sherif controlled the largest, most populous, and wealthiest part of Pakistan. The Punjab was also the home of the majority of the military. General Zia was from the Punjab and the strongest remaining supporters for what he stood for, Nawaz Sherif among them, were to be found in the Punjab. Prime Minister Bhutto and the Pakistan People's Party members in the provincial assembly tried to unseat Sherif and his Alliance Party but were outmaneuvered. As they were still recruiting votes for a no-confidence vote, Sherif caught them unprepared with a confidence vote which he won.

Despite the battles with Sherif and the religious right wing, Prime Minister Bhutto retained much of her popularity. Many Pakistanis were relieved by her secularization of government. They also enjoyed the apparent renaissance that was beginning in the arts in Pakistan. Early in 1989 a one-hour television gala featured the singing and dancing of the brother and sister team of Nazia and Zohaib. The religious conservatives dubbed the show un-Islamic and unsuccessfully tried to have the performers punished. The majority of the Pakistani population sighed a collective sigh of relief to have entertainment on the state-owned TV. The permissiveness of Prime Minister Bhutto's new government spawned other artistic endeavors as well.

In April 1989 it was announced that Prime Minister Bhutto would make an official visit to the United States in June of that year. The agenda for the visit would be one of discussing the situation in Afghanistan with President Bush. Prime Minister Bhutto would also address the United States Congress in an attempt to strengthen support for continued aid to Pakistan. After completing her official duties in Washington, Prime Minister Bhutto would be the commencement speaker at Harvard University.

As the first official state visit of the Bush presidency, Prime Minister Bhutto was treated lavishly when she arrived in Washington on June 6, 1989. Just prior to her arrival, the White House announced that President Bush would recommend that the United States sell Pakistan $68 million worth of anti-aircraft missiles. He also promised that the United States would increase the aid for Pakistan's war on drugs by $1.5 million to $7.2 million.

In their private talks President Bush and Prime Minister Bhutto deviated from the positions of their two immediate predecessors. Now that the Soviet Union had withdrawn from Afghanistan, both leaders supported a political solution between the Soviet-backed regime in Kabul and the

United States President George Bush and Prime Minister Bhutto are followed by their spouses as they enter a state dinner at the White House in honor of the prime minister and her husband.

Prime Minister Bhutto receives applause from the United States Congress before giving her speech in June 1989. Behind Ms. Bhutto are House Speaker Tom Foley, left, and Senator Robert Byrd.

United States– and Pakistan–backed mujahedin rebels. They also discussed the attempts by Pakistan to develop nuclear weapons. United States intelligence reports had indicated that Pakistan was going forward in its development of nuclear weapons. However, Prime Minister Bhutto told President Bush and the press that she was a strong supporter of halting the proliferation of nuclear weapons. Also, she hoped that the United States would use its influence to prevent a nuclear arms race in South Asia. President Bush needed to certify to the Congress that Pakistan did not have nuclear weapons or the Congress would deny any further aid payments to Pakistan.

Prime Minister Bhutto addressed many of the same issues when she spoke to a joint session of Congress on June 7, 1989. Many in the audience were impressed by her speech, and some members of Congress said her speech was more eloquent than most of the ones they hear. Prime Minister Bhutto told the Congress about the advances for democracy that she symbolized. She said that, "Everywhere the sun is setting on the day of the dictator, the generals are returning to the barracks." She also reassured Congress that she did not want to be a party to a nuclear arms race in South Asia. Her speech went a long way toward insuring the continuation of aid to Pakistan.

At the 338th Harvard University Commencement on June 9, 1989, Prime Minister Benazir Bhutto received an honorary doctor of laws degree and gave the commencement address. She called for the democratic countries of the world to help countries such as Pakistan as they struggle to offer people basic human rights and a democratic government. Twenty-five thousand people stood in the rain to listen to this 1973 graduate of Harvard, impressed by her oratory and her message.

Epilogue

As Benazir Bhutto completes her first year in office and this book was being sent to the typesetter, the political situation in Pakistan remains unsettled. In the fall of 1989, Benazir Bhutto and her coalition government faced a serious challenge from opposition leaders. The opposition was able to collect enough votes to call for a no-confidence vote in the National Assembly. If Prime Minister Bhutto's government lost the no-confidence vote, then President Ishaq Khan would be free to ask the opposition to form a new government. In the weeks preceding the vote, rumors circulated claiming that members of the National Assembly were offered as much as one million dollars to switch sides. The rumors of vote-buying were substantiated by Assembly members on both sides. On November 4, 1989, Prime Minister Bhutto won the no-confidence vote by a slim eleven votes in the 236-seat Assembly.

It soon became apparent that Ms. Bhutto had made a few deals of her own. Three opposition party members were given cabinet-level appointments within the Bhutto government in exchange for their support. It appears, at least for the time being, that Prime Minister Bhutto will continue in office and may now have quieted the opposition leaders enough to move forward.

The fact is that Benazir Bhutto and the Pakistan People's Party have had to spend much of their efforts trying to maintain their hold on the government. In many ways this has prevented Prime Minister Bhutto from enacting many of the reforms that she had promised in her election

campaign. In some ways, conditions within Pakistan have changed little in a year. Illiteracy, poverty, corruption, and drug trafficking still continue as serious problems. Looked at in another light, the first year of Benazir Bhutto's leadership is remarkable. Freedom and democracy, which General Zia had wiped out, have returned.

The military, which has taken over the country four times in its brief history, has stayed out of politics. Even in the face of the disruption caused by the no-confidence vote, the generals have remained quiet. The problems that faced Benazir Bhutto seemed insurmountable when she was elected in December 1988. With the no-confidence vote behind her, there is renewed hope among many in Pakistan that this amazing woman can begin to solve some of those problems.

Her first year in office has shown her to be a competent diplomat who has garnered respect for herself and her country among the leaders of the rest of the world. She has been especially successful in getting the United States to renew its pledge of financial support to Pakistan.

On January 25, 1990 Benazir Bhutto achieved another first. She became the first leader of a modern state to give birth to a child while in office. The seven-pound, eight-ounce baby girl, whom they named Bakhtawar, is the second child of Ms. Bhutto and her husband, Asif Ali Zardari.

Benazir Bhutto is doing the best she can with what seem to be nearly insurmountable obstacles in Pakistan. It is hoped that with time those same obstacles will be shrunk by her guidance.

For Further Reading

Amnesty International. *Islamic Republic of Pakistan: An Amnesty International Report Including the Findings of a Mission to Pakistan 25 April – 12 May 1976.* London: Amnesty International, 1977.

Amnesty International. *Pakistan: Human Rights Violations and the Decline of the Rule of Law, an Amnesty International Report.* London: Amnesty International, 1982.

Bhutto, Benazir. *Daughter of Destiny: An Autobiography.* New York: Simon and Schuster, 1989.

Burki, Shahid Javed. *Pakistan under Bhutto, 1971–1977.* New York: St. Martin's Press, 1980.

Mody, Piloo. *Zulfi My Friend.* Delhi (India): Thonson Press Ltd., 1973.

Mumtaz, Khawar, and Farida Shaheed, editors. *Women of Pakistan, Two Steps Forward, One Step Back?* London: Zed Books, 1987.

Index

J B Bhutto
Doherty, Katherine M.
Benazir Bhutto /

$13.90 06/03/91 ABX-5938